CHAPS!
A JINGLE JANGLE
CHRISTMAS

Book by
Jahnna Beecham and Malcolm Hillgartner

Vocal Arrangements by
Malcolm Hillgartner and Chip Duford

FOUNDED 1830

New York   Hollywood   London   Toronto

Book Copyright © 2007 by Jahnna Beecham & Malcolm Hillgartner

ALL RIGHTS RESERVED

CAUTION: Professionals and amateurs are hereby warned that CHAPS! A JINGLE JANGLE CHRISTMAS being fully protected under the copyright laws of the United States of America, the British Commonwealth, including Canada, and the other countries of the Copyright Union, is subject to a royalty, and anyone presenting the play without the consent of the owners or their authorized agents will be liable to the penalties by law provided.

Amateurs wishing to arrange for the production of [insert title here] must make application to SAMUEL FRENCH, INC., at 45 West 25th Street, New York, NY 10010-2751, giving the following particulars:

(1) The name of the town and theatre or hall in which the proposed production will be presented.
(2) The maximum seating capacity of the theatre or hall.
(3) Scale of ticket prices; and
(4) The number of performances intended and the dates thereof.

Upon receipt of these particulars SAMUEL FRENCH, INC., will quote the amateur terms and availability.

Stock royalty and availability quoted on application to SAMUEL FRENCH, INC., at 45 West 25th Street, New York, NY 10010-2751.

For all other rights than those stipulated above, apply to Beacon Artists Agency, 120 East 56th Street, Suite 540, NY 10022 Att: Patricia McLaughlin.

An orchestration consisting of Piano/conductor's score will be loaned two months prior to the production ONLY on receipt of the royalty quoted for all performances, the rental fee and a refundable deposit. The deposit will be refunded on the safe return to SAMUEL FRENCH, INC. of all materials loaned for the production.

No one shall commit or authorize any act or omission by which the copyright of, or the right to copyright, this play may be impaired.

No one shall make any changes in this play for the purposes of production.

Publication of this play does not imply availability for performance. Both amateurs and professionals considering a production are strongly advised in their own interests to apply to Samuel French, Inc., for written permission before starting rehearsals, advertising, or booking a theatre.

No part of this book may be reproduced, stored in a retrieval system, or transmitted in any form, by any means, now known or yet to be invented, including mechanical, electronic, photocopying, recording, videotaping, or otherwise, without the prior permission of the publisher.

Printed in U.S.A.
ISBN 978-0-573-63400-0

IMPORTANT BILLING AND CREDIT REQUIREMENTS

All producers of CHAPS! A JINGLE JANGLE CHRISTMAS *must* give credit to the author of the work in all programs distributed in connection with performances of the Work, and in all instances in which the title of the Work appears for the purposes of advertising, publicizing or otherwise exploiting a production thereof, including, without limitation, programs, souvenir books and playbills. The name of the Author *must* appear on a separate line in which no other matter appears, immediately following the title of the Work, and *must* be in size of type not less than 50% of the size used for the title of the Work.

Billing *must* be substantially as follows:

(NAME OF PRODUCER)

Presents

CHAPS! A JINGLE JANGLE CHRISTMAS (100%)

by
Jahnna Beecham & Malcolm Hillgartner (50% of title type)

Vocal Arrangements by Malcolm Hillgartner and Chip Duford (25%)

Parody lyrics in WAY OUT THERE by Harrison Long (25%)

SONGS

I'm An Old Cowhand by Johnny Mercer, Copyright © 1936 WB Music Corp.

Saltey's Fish 'n Chips by Malcolm Hillgartner, Copyright © 1995 Chaps! Publishing.

Howdy Partner by Malcolm Hillgartner, Copyright (C) 2007 Chaps! Publishing.

Wahoo! by Cliff Friend, parody lyrics by Harrison Long, Copyright © 1936 (Renewed) Desylva Brown & Henderson Music, Chappell & Co.

Jingle Jangle Jingle by Joseph Lilley & Frank Loesser, Copyright © Famous Music Company.

Toastie Oaties by Malcolm Hillgartner, Copyright © 1995 Chaps! Publishing.

I Want to Be a Cowboy's Sweetheart by Patsy Montana, Copyright © MCA Music.

The Ballad of Curly Joe by Tim Spencer & Roy Rogers, Copyright © 1943 (Renewed) American Music, Inc.

Cattle Call by Tex Owens, Copyright © Forster Music Publishing.

Tumblin Tumbleweeds by Bob Nolan, Copyright © (Renewed) Music of the West.

Come 'n Get It by Dickie Wells, Copyright © 1959 (Renewed) WB Music Corp.

Gunslinger by Leo Pober & Bud Freeman, Copyright © Vickers Music.

Ride, Cowboy, Ride by C. Allen, D. DeMarco & Rex Allen, Jr., Copyright © Boxer Music.

White Cliffs of Dover/Roundup in the Spring by Lane Burton & Walter Kent/Trad, Copyright © Walter Kent Music, Copyright © Shapiro Bernstein & Company, Inc.

Ragtime Cowboy Joe by Lewis F. Muir, Maurice Abrahams & Grant Clarke Copyright © 1942 (Renewed) Alfred Music Company, Inc., EMI Robbins Catalog, Inc., Tree Publishing.

Cool Water by Bob Nolan, Copyright © (Renewed) Music of the West.

Sioux City Sue by Ray Freedman & Dick Thomas, Copyright © 1945, 1973 (Renewed) Edwin H. Morris & Company A Division of MPL Communications, Inc, Capano Music.

Cigareets and Whusky arrangements by Malcolm Hillgartner, Copyright © 1995 Chaps! Publishing.

Duelin' Divas with apologies to G. Bizet, parody lyrics by Harrison Long Copyright © 1995 Chaps! Publishing.

Roving Cowboy by Bob Nolan, Copyright © (Renewed) Music of the West

All Rights Reserved
Used by Permission

Chaps! A Jingle Jangle Christmas was originally produced at the Artists Repertory Theatre's 1997-1998 season, Portland, OR, Allen Nause, Producing Artistic Director. The production was under the direction of Jon Kretzu, with the following cast and production team:

        ARCHIE................................Jim Caputo
        LESLIE............................Grant Byington
        MILES........................Gary Wayne Cash
        CLIVE...................................Alan King
        STAN.............................Douglas Mace
        MABEL..........................Susannah Mars

Set Designer – Lawrence Larsen
Costume Designer – Natalie Leavenworth
Lighting Designer – Jeff Forbes
Sound Designer – Martin John Gallagher
Prop Master – Roger Riecker
Music Director – Steve Dahlke
Choreographer – Gary Willis
Musicians – Ken Colburn (fiddle, accordion)
Joshua Tyree (guitar)
Stage Manager – Ann Yuhas

CAST

ARCHIE LEITCH — Cockney sound engineer, down-to-earth and quick with a quip. Plays the guitar, loves cowboy songs — and knows quite a few of them.

MILES SHADWELL — Intense young producer who's responsible for bringing the Singing Cowboys to Great Britain. If this holiday broadcast doesn't come off, he might as well kiss his job goodbye. If he wasn't so neurotic, he'd be a nice guy.

LESLIE BRIGGS-STRATTON — Imperious, arrogant snob of a BBC announcer á la George Sanders. Loathes cowboy songs. Is convinced he is civilization's last line of defense against the rise of vulgar populism on the radio. Nobody knows he was once a featured performer in music hall pantomime.

CLIVE COOPER — A radio personality of sorts, Clive IS the "Saltey's Fish 'n' Chips Man." An old school tie kind of guy, he really thinks of himself as a great AC-tor.

MABEL CARTER — Tex Riley's tour manager. Mabel is used to being a behind-the-scenes wallfower. But once she steps up to the mike, she's a rose in full bloom.

STAN — The sound effects man. Like Buster Keaton, this shell-shocked veteran is a man of few words.

THE SETTING

The year is 1944. The setting — Studio B at the BBC in London. A bold banner with a holly-and-mistletoe motif has been strung across the stage that reads:

SPECIAL HOLIDAY BROADCAST:
THE BBC WELCOMES AMERICA'S SINGING COWBOYS!

Four microphones are in place. A sound booth is off to one side. A sound effects station is stage left.

MUSICAL NUMBERS

Act One

1. I'm An Old Cowhand..*Archie*
2. Saltey's Fish 'n Chips...*Archie & Clive*
3. Howdy, Pardner!..*Archie, Mabel*
4. Wahoo!...*Leslie, Mabel, Archie*
5. Jingle Jangle Jingle Bells......................*Clive, Miles & Company*
6. I Want To Be A Cowboy's Sweetheart...........*Mabel, Miles, Clive*
7. The Ballad of Curly Joe.................................*Miles & Company*
8. Christmas on the Range.........................*Archie, Miles, Clive*
9. Cattle Call..*Mabel, Miles, Clive*
10. Tumblin Tumbleweeds..................*Archie, Mabel, Miles, Clive*
11. Come 'n Get It.......................................*Leslie & Company*
12. Gunslinger...............................*Clive, Archie, Miles, Leslie*
13. Ride, Cowboy, Ride...*Company*

Act Two

14. White Cliffs of Dover/I'll Be Home For Christmas..........*Mabel & Company*
15. Ragtime Cowboy Joe..*Company*
16. Cool Water..*Company*
17. Sioux City Sue.......................................*Clive, Miles, Mabel*
18. Cigareets and Whusky........................ *Archie, Clive, Miles*
19. I'm Gonna Tell Santy Claus On You.................*Leslie & Mabel*
20. Ragtime Cowboy Joe (Reprise)...................*Company*
21. Roving Cowboy/Ride Cowboy Ride........................*Company*

For Mary and David, for urging us to take this leap of faith; and Harrison and Chip, for helping us land it.

ACT I

(Lights come up in a tight spot on a man standing at microphone, in a military uniform, a cowboy hat, and a guitar, singing in a nice, easy cowboy drawl.)

ARCHIE.
STEP ASIDE, YOU ORNERY TENDERFEET,
LET A BIG BAD BUCKAROO PAST.
I'M THE TOUGHEST HOMBRE YOU'LL EVER MEET,
THO' I MAY BE THE LAST.
YES SIRREE, WE'RE A VANISHING RACE.
NO SIRREE, CAN'T LAST LONG.
STEP ASIDE, YOU ORNERY TENDERFEET,
WHILE I SING MY SONG.

I'M AN OLD COWHAND FROM THE RIO GRANDE,
BUT MY LEGS AIN'T BOWED, AND MY CHEEKS AIN'T
    TANNED.
I'M A COWBOY WHO NEVER SAW A COW,
NEVER ROPED A STEER 'CAUSE I DON'T KNOW HOW,
AN' I SURE AIN'T FIXIN' TO START IN NOW.
YIPPY-I-O-KI-

(ARCHIE breaks off, taps mike, talks to booth with a Cockney accent.)

ARCHIE. Tweak up the volume on the Sykes, will yer?

(LESLIE ENTERS, SR, sheaf of papers in hand.)

LESLIE. *(Going to announcer's podium DR.)* Sod off, Archie! I'm cuing up.

(Three tones chime, signaling announcement.)

O.S. VOICE FROM BOOTH. Leslie in five, four, three, two —

(ARCHIE moves to adjust SL mike but stops moving by end of count. ON AIR sign on wall flashes. Trace of music audible as selection playing ends.)

LESLIE. *(Into mike, hand on ear.)* That was our own Ray Noble and his Orchestra bringing you a touch of the Old West with "Silv'ry Rio Grande River, Stay 'Way from My Door." Don't forget to tune in later this hour for our special Christmas broadcast featuring Tex Riley and his Holiday Round-up, direct from America. I'm Leslie Briggs-Stratton, your humble presenter, and this *is* the BBC Home Service.

(Music swells, fades. ON AIR sign flashes off. ARCHIE slips a small screwdriver from a leather tool bag around his waist and adjusts the microphone. STAN, in uniform and helmet, enters carrying a SFX box.)

ARCHIE. *(Into mike.)* Testing, one, two —

(STAN trips and drops crash box.)

ARCHIE. Have yer got all the effects for the show, Stan?

(STAN makes loud, unruly noise with horn, and grins.)

LESLIE. *(Cringing, pressing hands to temples.)* Bloody hell.
ARCHIE. Too much 'oliday cheer last night, Les?
LESLIE. You have no idea.

(ARCHIE moves to next mike, and sings:)

ARCHIE.
I'M AN OLD COWHAND FROM THE RIO GRANDE
AND I COME TO TOWN JUST TO HEAR THE BAND.

O.S. WOMAN'S VOICE FROM BOOTH. You sound really good, Archie.

ARCHIE. Thanks, Alice.

O.S. VOICE FROM BOOTH. I almost believed you were one those cowboys from the silver screen. How do you do it?

ARCHIE. Nothin' to it, really. You just sort of shove yer voice up in yer nose, plant a silly smile on yer face, and let yer limbs go all wobbly-like.

(Sings again.)
I KNOW ALL THE SONGS THAT THE COWBOYS KNOW
ABOUT THE BIG CORRAL WHERE THE DOGIES GO

LESLIE.
'CAUSE YOU LEARNED THEM ALL ON THE RADIO.

ARCHIE.
YIPPEE-I-O-KI-YAY!

(STAN plays final YIPPEE-I-O-KI-YAY on SFX.
MILES SHADWELL rushes in from SR on final YAY, in a panic.)

MILES. Where are they? Have they arrived yet?
ARCHIE. 'Ave 'oo arrived?
MILES. The Americans.

(TONES chime.
ON AIR sign flashes on. MILES, ARCHIE & STAN freeze as RULE BRITANNIA fanfare plays.)

LESLIE. This is the BBC Home Service.

(Music fades; ON AIR sign flashes off.)

MILES. Our singing cowboys. *(Gestures to banner above bandstand.)* Tonight's Christmas broadcast!

O.S. WOMAN'S VOICE FROM BOOTH. Haven't heard a word, Miles. And we go in fifteen.
MILES. I've rung round to all the train stations and nobody has seen them.
LESLIE. No cowboys? Dear, dear. Whatever shall Auntie do?
ARCHIE. Watch yer step, Les, or Miles will dress you up in a silly 'at and make you go on.
MILES. This is a disaster. *(wheeze)* A royal disaster. *(another wheeze)* We've publicized it for weeks. What are we going to do?
LESLIE. What do you mean, *we*, old boy? Personally I was against the whole vulgar affair from the start.
MILES. Have you looked outside the studio? The queue for tonight's show runs completely 'round the block. *(Big wheeze.)*
LESLIE. Why's he wheezing like that?
ARCHIE. It's 'is asthma. It always acts up when 'e's agitated.
MILES. *(Wheeze!)*
LESLIE. Can't you do something to make him stop?
MILES. *(Wheeze!)*
ARCHIE. Now, Miles, don't get yer knickers in a twist. We've still got fifteen minutes. That's plenty of time. Isn't it, Leslie?
LESLIE. Have you lost your mind? Even if they did arrive in the next few minutes, they would have to set up, put on their costumes and tune their instruments...
MILES. You're happy they're not here.
LESLIE. I'm overjoyed.
MILES. You hope they don't make it.
LESLIE. *(Open-mouthed smile, big nod, meaning. "You got it.")*
MILES. You stinker! I don't feel well at all. The room is spinning. I think I'm going to be ill.

(MILE runs out with his hand over his mouth.)

LESLIE. *That's* our producer?
ARCHIE. Give 'im a chance, Les.
LESLIE. Whatever for? The only reason that fool's a producer is because all the really talented chaps are at the front, doing their bit for God and country.

(ARCHIE gives LESLIE a dour look.)

LESLIE. Don't give me that hero of Dunkirk look. You know I tried to enlist. Is it my fault my arches had fallen?
CLIVE. *(Off-stage)* Yoo-hoo! I say — Leslie!
LESLIE. Oh, goody. It's Clive Cooper.

(CLIVE pops his head in studio door. He's carrying a box full of brightly wrapped presents.)

CLIVE. Happy Christmas, everybody!
ARCHIE. It's the Saltey's Fish 'n Chips Man!

(CLIVE's button has been pushed and he automatically launches into a commercial.)

CLIVE. Puts a smile on your face, and a tingle in your tummy.

(ARCHIE strums the familiar chord; ARCHIE and CLIVE sing the Saltey's Fish 'n Chips jingle in music hall style. STAN accompanies them on SFX.)

CLIVE & ARCHIE.
HAVE A SALTEY'S FISH AND CHIPS TODAY.
THEY'RE EVER SO GOOD, EVER SO GRAND,
YOU FEEL JUST LIKE A MARCHING BAND
AND WHEN THE BUGLE CALLS, YOU'LL HEAR THEM SAY,
HAVE A SALTEY'S TODAY.

LESLIE. Don't call us. We'll call you.
CLIVE. *(Presents LESLIE with a gift.)* Here, Leslie.
LESLIE. For me? *(Opens the box, sees it's a Santa hat. He is not amused.)* You shouldn't have.
CLIVE. It's for the Christmas Broadcast. I thought you might — dear God! I almost forgot, there's a...there's a...there's a —

(The warning tones chime. ALL freeze as ON AIR sign flashes on.)

LESLIE. You've been listening to the Tinseltown Tubateers, under the baton of Gustav Phlegm. *(Clears throat slightly.)* This is the BBC Home Service.

(ON AIR sign flashes off.)

    CLIVE. GIRL!! Outside. Chilled to the bone. With something called the Holiday turn-over, er, roundabout, eh —
    ARCHIE. Round-up.
    CLIVE. No, that's not it. Holiday —
    LESLIE. Round-up.
    CLIVE. No, no, I've almost got it. Holiday... Holiday —
    ARCHIE & LESLIE. *(Shout)* ROUND-UP!!!!
    CLIVE. That's it.
    ARCHIE. So where's the girl?
    CLIVE. Oh. Right. The girl.

(CLIVE sets his packages, including one that's an obvious fifth of whisky, under the tree.)

    CLIVE. She's just out here.

(CLIVE & ARCHIE RUN OUT SL doors.)

    ARCHIE. *(As he follows CLIVE out.)* Is she pretty?

(LESLIE crosses R to announcer area, shuffles papers, preparing for his next announcement. STAN continues to decorate and check and set up SFX.
The BBC tones chime.
ENTER MABEL, from the house. She's freezing. MABEL is bundled up in a winter coat and mittens. She wears a cowboy hat. She sees LESLIE.)

    MABEL. Excuse me, sir?

(LESLIE holds up hand to silence MABEL as ON AIR sign flashes on.)

    LESLIE. Be sure and join us tomorrow evening for another thrilling broadcast of —

(SFX: organ music swell.)

LESLIE. *(Spoken in a lugubrious tone, ending with a mad laugh.)* Appointment With Fear. *(ON AIR flashes off. LESLIE grips his temples in "hangover" pain.)* Ow...
MABEL. Sir?
LESLIE. *(Looking over his next announcement.)* Good lord, who dangled this participle? *Miles!*
MABEL. Pardon me?

(MILES ENTERS, SR.)

LESLIE. This simply won't do. *(Sees MILES.)*Miles!
MILES. Not now, Leslie. *(To STAN.)* Where's Archie got to?

(STAN points off left.)

MABEL. *(To MILES.)* Can you help me?
MILES. Sorry, miss, but I'm extremely busy.

(MILES GOES OFF L. LESLIE starts to follow. Next two lines occur simultaneously.)

LESLIE. I can't possibly be expected to say these words —
MABEL. *(To STAN)* I'm with the Holiday Roundup.

(LESLIE pops right back in door, all ears.)

MABEL. I'm the tour manager. Have I come to the right place?

(STAN gestures to sign on bandstand, and rings a bell. Mabel is relieved. She divides her speech between STAN and LESLIE.)

MABEL. You would not believe what I have been through. It was snowing like crazy, and our train was late when we pulled into Victoria Station. I had to wait for the luggage, so Tex and the boys went on without me. I thought I wasn't going to make it. But here I am, and the show can go on.
LESLIE. Oh, goodie.

(CLIVE pulls trunk in from SL, ARCHIE at other end, MILES follows.)

CLIVE. I'm certain this is her trunk. Ask her if you don't believe me. *(Spots MABEL.)* There she is!

(MILES rushes over.)

MILES. Miss Carter! At last! Welcome to Broadcasting House. I'm your producer, Miles Shadwell.
MABEL. *(Shakes hands.)* Am I glad to see you!
ARCHIE. *(Extends hand.)* I'm yer sound man, Archie Leitch. Pleased to meet you.
CLIVE. Clive Cooper. H'actor. *(Kisses her hand.)* Enchanté.
LESLIE. *(Curt nod.)* Leslie Briggs-Stratton.
CLIVE. Staff announcer. *(Drops voice.)* Stuffed shirt.

(STAN crawls out from beneath the SFX table to retrieve a fallen item. He crawls back under as MILES says:)

MILES. That's Stan. He was in the War.
CLIVE. Still is.
MILES. Welcome to London, Miss Carter.
MABEL. Please, call me Mabel.
MILES. *(Overjoyed with relief.)* I was afraid the Holiday Round-up wasn't going to make it on the air. But we've still got ten minutes. So if you'll just bring in Mr. Riley, we can set up —
MABEL. *(Cuts in.)* Mr. Riley? Isn't Tex here?
MILES. No. I thought he was with you.
MABEL. No. He was supposed to be here.
MILES. Well, he's not.
MABEL. Well, where is he?
MILES. How should I know?
MABEL. Well, you're the producer!
MILES. Well, you're the tour manager.
MABEL. I don't believe it. I don't believe it. I was at the station, I said, you go on ahead. I'll wait here for the props and the...and the... *(Looks at LESLIE and gestures.)*...you know.

LESLIE. *(Interprets)* Costumes?
MABEL. Yes. I took the very next cab that came into the station. I thought they'd be here in the studio, you know... *(Mimes playing the guitar.)*
LESLIE. *(Right in there.)* Warming up.
MABEL. Yes, but...but...but — *(Makes a "heckfire" gesture with arm.)*
LESLIE. *(With relish.)* Heckfire — they're not.

(MABEL puts her face in her hands.)

MABEL. *(Gasps)* Ohhhh...
LESLIE. *(Mimes taking off a hat.)* It's a sad day on the range for all of us.
MILES. This is a complete disaster.
CLIVE. What are you going to do?
MILES. *(Beat)* Panic! *(Wheeze)*
MABEL. I don't believe it. I've lost my cowboys.
MILES. You've lost your cowboys *(Wheeze)* — and I'm about to lose my job.
CLIVE. Steady on, old chap.
MILES. *(Grabs CLIVE by the collar.)* Do you have any idea what's at stake here?
CLIVE. Not really, no.
MILES. In less than ten minutes all of Great Britain, as well as our troops at the front, will be tuning in for our special Christmas Broadcast — and what will they hear?
LESLIE. *(Hopefully)* Me, reading the yuletide sermons of Bishop Ramsbottom.
MILES. They want cowboys, Leslie. Can you be a cowboy?
LESLIE. Get stuffed.
MILES. Well, *somebody* has to be a cowboy. That's what we promised our listeners, and that's what they'll bloody well get.
LESLIE. If it's a cowboy you're looking for, talk to Archie. He's an old cowhand.
ARCHIE. Sorry?
MILES. That's right. You were singing when I came in. For a moment I actually thought you were with the Holiday Roundup.

(MABEL takes a closer look at ARCHIE.)

MABEL. You know, you could almost pass for Tex.
ARCHIE. Me?

(MABEL places her cowboy hat on ARCHIE's head.)

MABEL. *(To MILES.)* What do you think?
MILES. *(Whispers excitedly.)* It just might work.
ARCHIE. What?
MABEL. I know the show backwards and forwards. I've got the scripts and the sheet music. No one would ever know.
LESLIE. Except the studio audience.
MABEL. But I have the costumes.
MILES. Most of our people have never seen Tex or any of the all-star cowboys in the flesh.
MABEL. Why, you can slap a ten gallon hat on anyone and make 'em look like a cowboy. *(To LESLIE, who's taking a long swig of "tea.")* Even you.
LESLIE. Now hold on! That's *not* in my contract.
MILES. Contract? All of our contracts will be terminated if we don't broadcast this Christmas special.
LESLIE. Don't be absurd. It's just a lot of silly cowboy music.
MILES. Well, it so happens the director-general *likes* silly cowboy music. The one thing he does *not* like is excuses. So if we don't have four cowboys singing their silly Christmas songs in front of that microphone in five minutes, the ax will fall. And it won't be just my head that rolls. I'll take you down with me, Leslie — I swear I will.
LESLIE. Is that a threat?
MILES. *(Barks)* Yes!
LESLIE. Oh. *(Beat)* In that case, I'm in.
MILES. And so am I. Archie? Can I count on you?
ARCHIE. *(Gulps)* I'm game.
MILES. Clive?
CLIVE. Well...I s'pose I could h'act the part. After all, that's what I do — h'act. I mean, for eight years, I've been the Saltey's Fish 'n Chips Man. *(Does slogan.)* "Puts a smile on your face and a tingle in your tummy." But as for the singing part...

MABEL. I'll work with you, Clive, you'll be fine. Can you boys do this?

(Sings)
YIPPEE-YAY!

(Points to ARCHIE, who sings the 3rd.)

ARCHIE.
YIPPEE-YAY!

(MABEL points to MILES, who sings the 5th.)

MILES.
YIPPEE-YAY!

(MABEL points to CLIVE, who sings the 7th.)

CLIVE.
YIPPEE-YAY!

(The chord stacks up perfectly. MABEL points to LESLIE, who won't sing.)

LESLIE. *(Snottily)* Yippee-yay.

(Slow burn to LESLIE from ALL.)

MILES. *(Grimly)* Five minutes. We have five minutes to teach Leslie how to sing.
LESLIE. *(Rushes to table for another drink.)* Dear God. I need another cup of tea. Make that a double.

(MILES, ARCHIE & CLIVE remember LESLIE's little drinking problem. It's an appalling thought.)

MILES. Oh, no, we've got to keep him off the sauce.

ARCHIE. Bloody well right.
CLIVE. Remember what happened last time.
MABEL. Last time?
ARCHIE. You don't want to know.
MABEL. Oh dear. I'll pass out the scripts while you fellas get dressed.
MILES. Where are the costumes?
MABEL. In that trunk. The others are in the lobby, with the musicians. *(Wide-eyed.)* Musicians! We've got to get them in here.
MILES. I'll do it.

(MILES EXITS. CLIVE opens trunk and picks out a few costume pieces.)

CLIVE. I'll take one of those. And one of those. And a couple of those.

(ARCHIE puts on a Stetson, gestures with hands like six-shooters.)

ARCHIE. Stick 'em up.
CLIVE. Is that one of those 10-pint hats?
LESLIE. That's 10-gallon, you imbecile.

(MABEL sets sheet music on music stand SC.)

MABEL. We don't have time to work through all of the numbers, so I'll run through the openings with you and then we'll just...wing it.

(LESLIE pulls out the Act Two dresses — MABEL's, and the red one he will wear as BELLE.)

LESLIE. I say. Who's supposed to wear these?

(ALL stare at MABEL.)

MABEL. Oh, my gosh. I forgot about Polly and Molly.
CLIVE. Polly and Molly?

MABEL. The sweethearts of the radio. What are we going to do?
ARCHIE. Why don't you play their parts?
MABEL. But I'm the stage manager. I can't perform.
LESLIE. *(Holds out a dress.)* Listen, duckie — if I'm going on, *you're* going on.
MABEL. But...

(TONES for announcement. ALL freeze as ON AIR sign flashes on. LESLIE steps to mike.)

LESLIE. Stay tuned for a special Christmas show you won't want to miss. Live from Broadcasting House — it's Tex Riley and his Holiday Round-up, coming to you in three minutes.

(ON AIR flashes off.)

ALL. Three minutes!
MABEL. *(Desperate)* All right, I'll do it!

(LESLIE tosses her the dress. ARCHIE, LESLIE & CLIVE jam up the exit, yelling at once.)

CLIVE. Costume! I need a costume!
ARCHIE. I've got to tune me guitar.
LESLIE. I can't do anything without a script.
MABEL. There's just one teensy little problem.
ARCHIE. It's all right, luv, we'll 'andle it.
MABEL. No, really, it's just that ...
LESLIE. Out of my *way!*

(THEY explode through the exit and are gone. MABEL is left alone on stage holding the two dresses.)

MABEL. —Polly and Molly sing a duet.

BLACK OUT

(Important note: From act one, scene 2 until the end of the play, this is a live radio broadcast. The theatre audience becomes the studio audience. The actors must always be aware that someone is watching them, while also staying aware of the greater "radio" audience listening through the microphones. To maintain the illusion of a live studio broadcast, the actors must hold scripts, or script pages, in hand whenever possible, and refer to those scripts often.

The microphones should be "live," i.e., amplified over the theatre sound system.

Unless otherwise indicated, all lines should be spoken into the mikes.

When speaking "off mike" for asides, the actors should cover the mike with their hands, or indicate with business that they are aware of the live mike and are trying to cover.

Also, regarding when and when not to use British accents, we've found that "Beatles rule" tends to work well — when the lads are singing, they sound American; when they speak, they sound British. The only exception is LESLIE, who speaks and sings in proper English.)

Scene 2

(During the blackout, the William Tell Overture is played; MUSICIANS get in place on bandstand. Spot comes up on SR mike. No one is there.

Blackout. William Tell Overture plays again. Lights come up. MILES sticks his head out from SR.)

MILES. Leslie?

(Blackout. William Tell Overture plays a third time, in an even higher key. When the spot comes up again, MILES is discovered standing at the SR mike, script in hand. He's in his cowboy shirt and boxer shorts.)

MILES. Good evening...and welcome to you in our studio audience, and all of the troops abroad. This special holiday broadcast is coming to you live from Portland Place, London —

(*MILES realizes he's in his shorts, and is seized with a violent asthma attack. CLIVE, in partial cowboy costume, rushes onstage, snatches away the script and pushes MILES off stage. MABEL is in costume [it was under her coat] and setting scripts on music stands onstage. When MILES mentions POLLY, she waves one hand. And on MOLLY, she waves the other.)*

CLIVE. Have we got a show for you tonight. This evening's programme features the zany antics of Slappy Burdette, the comic hijinks of Jack and Aces, the vocal stylings of the lovely Polly — and Molly — and an exciting episode from the adventures of Cowboy Joe and his Lonesome Rangers. The star of tonight's Radio Round-up is America's favorite singing cowboy. Millions of devoted fans already know and love him from his many recordings and popular action films. *(CLIVE gasps, covers mike, and whispers to MABEL)* My word, they've all seen him at the pictures. They'll know it's not him. What shall I say?
MABEL. Make something up. *(EXITS to get "TEX".)*
CLIVE. *(Back into mike.)* And...and here in his first public performance since contracting that, er, disfiguring disease...let's give a hearty John Bull welcome to the trail boss of tonight's Holiday Round-up — Tex Riley!

MUSIC INTRO: *"HOWDY, PARDNER!"*

(APPLAUSE LIGHT FLASHES.
ARCHIE ENTERS from UL door, crosses to C mike in cowboy hat, vest and chaps, playing guitar. He's got his own kind of stage fright. CLIVE EXITS, a wrung-out wreck. MABEL has followed ARCHIE onstage, hovers nearby to help.)

ARCHIE.
HOWDY, PARDNER, GLAD YOU CAME ALONG
THE HANDLE'S TEX, AND I'M HERE TO SING A SONG
OF CATTLE DRIVES AND STARRY NIGHTS
OUT UPON THE TRAIL, DAYS IN THE SADDLE
OUT WHERE THE COYOTES WAIL.

HOWDY, PARDNER, I KINDA LIKE YOUR STYLE.

LET'S GATHER ROUND THE CAMPFIRE FOR A WHILE.
WE'LL TELL A TALE OR TWO,
AND WHEN OUR TIME IS THROUGH,
WE'LL HIT THE DUSTY TRAIL WITH A SMILE!

(When he sings, ARCHIE sounds like Tex but when he speaks, his native Cockney returns in full force. MABEL holds the script in front of ARCHIE.)

ARCHIE. *(Reads)* Merry Christmas to all you folks in jolly old England. Y'know, ridin' 'erd on a string o' words is a bit off me range — partickerly when I'm speaking ta so many of yers all at once. But I do wanna say 'owdy real friendly-like and let you know just how pleased I am to be 'ere. *(Gives up.)* Aw, blimey, I guess me ol' guitar can say it better' n' I can.

MABEL. *(Aside)* You can say that again.

ARCHIE & MABEL.
YIPPEE-KI-YI-YOU!
NO MATTER WHAT THE WEATHER,
WE'LL RIDE IT OUT TOGETHER, ME AND YOU.

YIPPEE-KI-YI-YEE!
WITH ALL THE STARS TO GUIDE US,
OUR SADDLE PALS BESIDE US,
LET'S SERENADE THE DOGIES WITH SOME PRAIRIE HARMONY.

HOWDY, PARDNER, GLAD YOU CAME MY WAY
LET'S RAISE A RUCKUS, HAVE A LAUGH AND PLAY,
WE'LL ROSIN UP THE BOW
AND TUNE THE OL' BANJO,
TEX RILEY AND THE BOYS ARE HERE TODAY!

(APPLAUSE LIGHT.
ARCHIE and MABEL shake hands, relieved that they got through the song. MABEL hands script to ARCHIE.)

ARCHIE. *(Reads)* Thank you, everyone for that warm welcome. And now I'm pleased to introduce to you Miss...

MABEL. *(Speaks quickly into mike.)* Polly.
ARCHIE. Polly?
MABEL. Molly.
ARCHIE. Miss Polly Molly. *(Looks at her, confused.)*
MABEL. But you can call me Mabel.
ARCHIE. All right...Mabel. She's the sweetheart of this rodeo so let's give her a big hand.

(APPLAUSE LIGHT.)

MABEL. Um, thanks, Tex. Merry Christmas, everybody! You don't know how glad I am to be here.
ARCHIE. *(Fervently)* You don't know how glad we are to have you here — *(Catches himself.)* — to present this, er, show, to all the lads at the front.
MABEL. The front? *(To ARCHIE.)* My brother Bo is at the front. He's a corporal in the 1st Armored Division.
ARCHIE. *(Gestures at mike.)* Well, say hello.
MABEL. Bo? You listening out there? This is your sis, Mabel. I just want you to know how proud I am of you. Merry Christmas, Bo. You're in my heart and in my prayers.
ARCHIE. *(Back on script.)* Thank you, Mabel. And now, ladies and gents, let's get on with the show!

(SFX: Galloping hooves; horse whinnies; crash box.)

MABEL. *(Reads)* Who could that be, Tex?
ARCHIE. *(Reads)* Why, that sounds like me ol' pal, Slappy Burdette.

(They both make a sweeping gesture to the UR door. No one ENTERS. MILES pokes his head out the UL entrance.)

ARCHIE. *(Aside to MILES, under his breath.)* Where's Slappy?
MILES. *(Hisses)* I'll go find him. *(Runs to SR door, opens it and stage whispers offstage.)* Slappy? Pssst! Slappy, you're on.
LESLIE. *(Off-stage.)* How am I doing?

(MILES EXITS through door.)

ARCHIE. *(Tries to cover, into mike.)* Why, there you are, Slappy. Come over 'ere and sing us a song.
LESLIE. *(Off-stage.)* I'd rather not.
ARCHIE. *(Brightly)* Aw, come on, Slappy. The folks're countin' on you. *(Crosses to door, hisses.)* And so am I! Now get your arse out 'ere or I'll bring it out meself! *(EXITS through door.)*

MUSIC INTRO: *"WAHOO"*

(A miserable LESLIE appears in chaps, bowler and gaudy Christmas vest. He snatches the page of script from MABEL and marches to center, flanked by MABEL (L) and ARCHIE (R).)

LESLIE. *(Flatly)* Yippee-i-o-ki-yay.

(MABEL and ARCHIE usher LESLIE down to center mike.)

MABEL. Ki-yippee, Slappy!
LESLIE. Ki-yippee-what?
ARCHIE. *(Clenched teeth.)* Ki-yippee-*sing*!

(LESLIE recites the lines in an archly sonorous tone. He sings on the choruses, and during the last verse.)

LESLIE.
WAY OUT WEST WHERE MEN ARE MEN
AND WOMEN ARE VERY SWEET,
THAT'S WHERE I WANT TO BE,
THAT'S WHERE I'M GOING TO BE.

WAY OUT WEST, JUST ONCE AGAIN,
WHERE HAPPINESS IS COMPLETE,
THERE IS ONE THING I MISS
AND IT IS THIS.

LESLIE, ARCHIE & MABEL.
OH, GIMME A HORSE, A GREAT BIG HORSE,
GIMME A BUCKAROO, AND LET ME

LESLIE. Wahoo, wahoo, wa-hoo.

ALL.
OH, GIMME A RANGE, A BIG FAT RANGE,
GIMME A STETSON, TOO, AND LET ME

LESLIE. Wahoo, wahoo, wa-hoo.

ALL.
GIVE ME THE WIDE OPEN SPACES.

MABEL.
I'M JUST LIKE A PRAIRIE FLOWER,

ARCHIE.
GROWING WILDER BY THE HOUR.

ALL.
GIVE ME A MOON, A PRAIRIE MOON,
GIVE ME A GAL THAT'S TRUE AND LET ME

LESLIE. Wahoo, wahoo, wa-hoo!

(LESLIE coyly folds the script and puts it away; a malicious grin on his face as he improvises the next verse.)

LESLIE.
Way out west, in the dusty west
Where the cowboys never bathe,
That's where I'd never roam
because it makes me groan.

To go back home, just once again
Where civilized people dwell
And they don't smell,
Would be so swell.

(SINGS)
OH, GIVE ME A FLASK, A SPOT OF TEA,

GIVE ME A CRUMPET, TOO AND LET ME
WA-HOO, WA-HOO, WAHOO.

OH, GIVE ME A PUB, SOME ENGLISH GRUB
JUST ONE LITTLE PINT OF BREW
AND LET ME WA-HOO, WA-HOO, WAHOO.

(ARCHIE and MABEL cut LESLIE off.)

    ARCHIE & MABEL.
GIVE ME THE WIDE OPEN SPACES

    MABEL.
I'M JUST LIKE A PRAIRIE FLOWER

    ARCHIE.
GROWING WILDER BY THE HOUR

    ALL.
GIVE ME A MOON, A PRAIRIE MOON,
GIVE ME A GAL THAT'S TRUE
AND LET ME WA-HOO, WA-HOO, WA-HOO

WA-HOO, WA-HOO —

(SFX: Duck Quacks.)

WA — HOO!

(APPLAUSE LIGHT.)

    LESLIE. Drink! I need a drink!

(MABEL shoots ARCHIE a warning look.)

    ARCHIE. *(Aside)* I'll get the bottle.

(During MABEL's intro, ARCHIE beats LESLIE to the table, grabs bottle and hides it behind screen. LESLIE pulls out a hip flask and tosses back a stiff one behind ARCHIE's back.)

MUSIC INTRO: *"JACK O'DIAMONDS THEME"*

MABEL. Now, ladies and gents, we have a real treat for you tonight. Here in Studio B are those two comical stars of the Silver Screen, Jack Diamond and his sidekick —

(CLIVE ENTERS SR, looking like a rhinestone cowboy, an oversized 10-gallon hat on his head, and doing his best cowboy acting job.)

CLIVE. *(Into mike.)* Howdy, pardners. It shore is good to be ridin' the radio range. You know, after a hard day of lassoing, I like to relax with me ol' geetar — *(Kicks into automatic pitch.)* And a nice plate of Saltey's Fish 'N Chips. "Puts a smile on your face and a tingle in your tummy." (*MABEL shoots him a look and he gets back on track.*) And since me name *is* Jack Diamond, I'd like to sing a little ditty of the same name.
MABEL. Excuse me, Jack, but aren't you forgetting something?
CLIVE. *(Checks fly.)* Don't believe so. Nope.
MABEL. Heh-heh-heh, you are such a card. I'm talking about your sidekick, Aces.
CLIVE. Aces?
MABEL. Yes. The little fellow with the wooden head?
CLIVE. Oh?

(ARCHIE grabs dummy from trunk, hands it to MABEL.)

CLIVE. *(Sees dummy.)* Oh, *that* Aces.

(MABEL tosses dummy to CLIVE, who accidentally pulls the dummy's head off while catching it.)

CLIVE. I—I thought I'd do a solo act tonight.

(CLIVE tosses dummy back to MABEL; keeps the head.)

MABEL. You never do a solo act, Jack.

(MABEL tosses dummy to CLIVE low; he tosses head to MABEL high.)

CLIVE. Never?
MABEL. *Never.*

(MABEL tosses head to CLIVE; now he has both head and body.)

CLIVE. Well, then, I guess I'll have to rustle up a dummy.

(MILES pops head in UR door.)

MILES. *(Stage whisper.)* Is anything wrong?

(CLIVE grabs MILES.)

CLIVE. You'll do.
MILES. What — me? No!

(Scuffle as CLIVE hustles MILES behind screen upstage. MABEL cues the BAND to vamp, as ARCHIE and LESLIE joins CLIVE behind screen. MILES is changed into dummy suit behind the screen.)

MABEL. *(In mike, covering.)* Boy, are we happy to have Jack Diamond and his sidekick Aces with us tonight.

(A squeal from MILES, his hat flies above the SCREEN. MABEL looks over shoulder, tries to keep covering.)

MABEL. You all remember these saddle pals from their terrific films, uh, Chip Off the Old Block —

(Another squawk, the dummy's clothes are tossed above SCREEN.)

MABEL. — and, uh, Saddle Splinters and, um, er —

(Another yelp, the unclothed dummy flies above the SCREEN. MABEL leaves mike, marches over to USL corner of SCREEN.)

MABEL. *(Hisses).* Do I need to remind you boys that we are live?
CLIVE. *(Pops head around SCREEN, stage whispers.)* It's all his fault. He won't be the dummy.
MABEL. Miles, didn't you say your job is on the line?
MILES. *(Pops head above SCREEN.) Job?*

(MILES, now dressed as the dummy, emits a high-pitched squeal as CLIVE and ARCHIE carry him by the arms and set him down on stool set by MABEL at center mike. MILES is in overdrive and, driven by adrenalin, bullets through the next section of jokes, laughing wildly at his own punchlines. CLIVE grabs script.)

MILES. Yoo-hoo. Yoo-hoo. Jack. I say, Jack.
CLIVE. *(Searching script.)* Yes, Aces, what is it?
MILES. *(At breakneck speed.)* A man was terribly fond of plums. He had plums for breakfast, plums for lunch, plums for tea, plums for dinner. He always walked along the street eating plums, had his pockets full of them, ate them in the train, in the pictures — even ate them in bed. *(Looks at CLIVE.)* What was his wife's name?
CLIVE. *(Mystified)* I don't know, what?
MILES. Victoria. You thought I was going to say Mrs. Plummer, didn't you. *(Laughs wildly.)*
MABEL. *(Aside to ARCHIE.)* What should we do? Miles is out of control.
MILES. My parents say I don't what good clean fun is. And they're right. *(Turns to CLIVE.)* I don't know what good it is.

(CLIVE desperately tries to get back to the script.)

CLIVE. Ha-ha, that's all very funny but don't you think we should —?
MILES. *(To CLIVE.)* Did you hear about poor Reggie?
CLIVE. *(Gamely)* No, what about poor Reggie?
MILES. He drowned in a vat of beer. Terrible, terrible. Took over an hour.
CLIVE. Oh, dear. What happened?

MILES. Well, you know Reggie works up at the Slipshod Brewery and he just leaned over too far and fell right into that vat of beer.
CLIVE. But why did it take an hour for him to drown?
MILES. He had to get out three times to go to the 'loo.

(SFX: "Pa-dump-pump" rim shot from STAN.)

ARCHIE. *(Aside)* Oh, no. 'E's doing every bad joke 'e's ever 'eard.
MABEL. *(Aside)* We've got to shut him up.
LESLIE. *(Aside)* Why don't we shoot him?
MILES. *(Yelling)* Hello, Jack! I'm calling you from the North Pole.
CLIVE. *(Shouting back.)* Why are you shouting?
MILES. No phone!
MABEL. That does it!

(MABEL picks up a tambourine and cues the BAND to start the:)

MUSIC INTRO: *"JINGLE, JANGLE, JINGLE BELLS"*

MILES. I say, Jack, what's that sound?
CLIVE. *(Thrilled to find this cue in the script.)* That sounds like the cue for a song.
MILES. Song! What song? I don't know any —
CLIVE. It's MY song!

(CLIVE claps his hand over MILES' mouth as MABEL, ARCHIE and LESLIE sing.)

MABEL, ARCHIE & LESLIE.
YIPPEE YAY, THERE'LL BE NO WEDDING BELLS FOR TODAY.

CLIVE. (MILES.)
I'VE GOT SPURS THAT JINGLE, JANGLE, JINGLE,
AS I GO RIDING MERRILY ALONG.
AND THEY SING,

OH, AIN'T YOU GLAD YOU'RE SINGLE,
AND THAT SONG AIN'T SO VERY FAR FROM WRONG.

OH, LILY BELLE (OH, LILY BELLE),
OH, LILY BELLE (OH, LILY BELLE),
THOUGH I MAY HAVE DONE SOME FOOLIN'
THIS IS WHY I NEVER (WHY I NEVER) FELL.

I GOT SPURS THAT JINGLE JANGLE JINGLE
AS I GO RIDING MERRILY ALONG
AND THEY SING, OH, AIN'T YOU GLAD YOU'RE SINGLE
AND THAT SONG AIN'T SO VERY FAR FROM WRONG

OH, MARY ANNE (OH, MARY ANNE)
OH, MARY ANNE (OH MARY ANNE)
THOUGH I'VE DONE SOME MOONLIGHT WALKING
THIS IS WHY I UP AND (WHY I UP AND) RAN

I GOT SPURS THAT JINGLE, JANGLE, JINGLE,
(JINGLE BELLS, JINGLE BELLS)
AS I GO RIDING MERRILY ALONG,
(MERRY CHRISTMAS!)
AND THEY SING, OH, AIN'T YOU GLAD YOU'RE SINGLE,
(I'M ECSTATIC!)
AND THAT SONG AIN'T SO VERY FAR FROM WRONG.

(MILES takes this chorus, the BAND stops after 2nd Bessie Lou.)

    MILES.
OH, BESSIE LOU, OH, BESSIE LOU!

(MILES at a loss for words, makes them up.)

    MILES.
JINGLE, JINGLE, JINGLE,
JANGLE... TWENTY-THREE SKIDOO!

(The BAND comes back in and MILES throws himself into JINGLE BELLS; CLIVE struggles to keep up.)

MILES.
DASHING THROUGH THE SNOW
IN A ONE HORSE OPEN SLEIGH,
O'ER THE FIELDS WE GO
LAUGHIN' ALL THE WAY, HA HA HA!

BELLS ON BOBTAIL RING
MAKING SPIRITS BRIGHT,
WHAT FUN IT IS TO RIDE AND SING
A SLEIGHING SONG TONIGHT.
    CLIVE. (MILES.)
OH SALLY JANE (OH SALLY JANE)
OH SALLY JANE (OH SALLY JANE)
THOUGH I'D LOVE TO STAY FOREVER
THIS IS WHY I CAN'T (WHY I CAN'T) REMAIN

I GOT SPURS THAT JINGLE, JANGLE, JINGLE
(JINGLE BELLS, JINGLE BELLS, JINGLE ALL THE WAY)
AS I GO RIDIN' MERRILY ALONG
(OH, WHAT FUN IT IS TO RIDE IN A ONE HORSE OPEN
    SLEIGH.)

AND THEY SAY, HEY, AIN'T YOU GLAD YOU'RE SINGLE
(JINGLE BELLS, JINGLE BELLS, JINGLE ALL THE WAY)
AND I CAN'T HARDLY SAY THAT THEY ARE —
(OH, WHAT FUN IT IS TO RIDE IN A)

    MILES & CLIVE.
ONE HORSE OPEN —
JINGLIN'-A-JANGLIN'-A —
ONE HORSE OP-EN SLEIGH!!

(APPLAUSE LIGHT.)

    ARCHIE. Thanks, boys, that was real...purty. *(Can't find his place in script.)* Now, er, where were we?
    MABEL. You were about to sing us your favorite song, Tex.

ARCHIE. *(Covering)* They're all my favorites. Which one did you have in mind?

MABEL. *(Covers mike, whispers.)* Page six.
ARCHIE. *(Covers mike, whispers.)* I haven't got a page six.
MABEL. Uh, um, er — how 'bout you, Slappy? Have you got a favorite page six?
LESLIE. Fresh out, I'm afraid.
MABEL. Jack?
CLIVE. Sorry.
MABEL. Aces?

(ACES opens mouth.)

ACES. There once was a girl from Nantucket —

(CLIVE claps hand over MILES' mouth.)

CLIVE. It's back to you, Mabel.
MABEL. Oh. OK. Here's one of *my* favorites. *(Cues the Band, who start to play.)*

MUSIC INTRO:
"I WANT TO BE A COWBOY'S SWEETHEART"

MABEL.
YODEL CHORUS

I WANT TO BE A COWBOY'S SWEETHEART,
I WANT TO LEARN TO ROPE AND TO RIDE,
I WANT TO RIDE O'ER THE PLAINS AND THE DESERTS
OUT WEST OF THE GREAT DIVIDE.

I WANT TO HEAR THE COYOTES HOWLIN'
WHILE THE SUN SINKS IN THE WEST;
I WANT TO BE A COWBOY'S SWEETHEART,
THAT'S THE LIFE I LOVE THE BEST.

YODEL CHORUS. (Add MILES.)

MABEL.
I WANT TO RIDE OL' PAINT, GOIN' AT A RUN,
I WANT TO FEEL THE WIND IN MY FACE,
A THOUSAND MILES FROM THESE CITY LIGHTS
GOIN' A COWHAND'S PACE.

I WANT TO PILLOW MY HEAD NEAR THE SLEEPIN' HERD
WHILE THE MOON SHINES DOWN FROM ABOVE,
I WANT TO STRUM MY GUITAR AND YODEL-AY-DE-HOO,
OH, THAT'S THE LIFE THAT I LOVE.

YODEL CHORUS. *(Add CLIVE.)*

(Fiddler plays some "taters" and the BAND kicks in to double time; MABEL and Boys follow.)

MABEL.
I WANT TO BE A COWBOY'S SWEETHEART,
I WANT TO LEARN TO ROPE AND TO RIDE,
I WANT TO RIDE O'ER THE PLAINS AND THE DESERTS
OUT WEST OF THE GREAT DIVIDE.

I WANT TO HEAR THE COYOTES HOWLIN'
WHILE THE SUN SINKS IN THE WEST;
I WANT TO BE A COWBOY'S SWEETHEART,
THAT'S THE LIFE I LOVE THE BEST.

ALL.
YODEL CHORUS *(TWICE)*

(APPLAUSE LIGHT.
SFX: a fusillade of rapid-fire gun shots. CLIVE and MILES, MABEL read from script for next scene; CLIVE puts on dummy gloves.)

CLIVE. Take cover, Aces!
MILES. Help, Mabel, ya gotta hide me.
MABEL. From who?
MILES. Black Bart.

MABEL. Black Bart? What did you boys do to get him riled up?
CLIVE. Well, last Christmas me and Aces were playing a friendly game of five card draw —
MILES. — and I was dealing.
CLIVE. Then right in the middle of the best hand I ever had —
MILES. —I got seenus trouble.
MABEL. Seenus trouble? Don't you mean, sinus?
MILES. No, seenus. You see, I dealt from the bottom —
CLIVE. —and Bart seenus.

(ALL do a vaudeville "pa-dum-bump" to house.)

MILES. For a second there I thought we were going to wind up like Old Curly Joe from Idaho.
MABEL. What happened to him?

MUSIC INTRO: *"CURLY JOE FROM IDAHO"*

(CLIVE manipulates the dummy's hands from behind MILES, who works the feet as they act out the song.)

MILES.
LET ME TELL YOU A TALE OF A GAMBLIN' MAN,
THE ROUGHEST AND TOUGHEST OF ALL.
HE WAS OLD CURLY JOE FROM IDAHO,
HE WAS ROUGH AND RUGGED AND TALL.
HE WAS OVER SIX FEET AND AS SLIM AS A RAIL,
AND HIS EYES WERE AS BLACK AS THE NIGHT.
AND WHEN HE CUT LOOSE, THAT ORNERY CAYUSE
WOULD ALWAYS END UP IN A FIGHT.

ONE NIGHT HE STORMED INTO OL' BOOTHEEL SALOON
AND ROARED IN A VOICE BIG AND LOUD,
C'MON, EVERYONE, WE'RE IN FOR SOME FUN,
I'LL BUY THE DRINKS FOR THE CROWD.
NOW THE GAMBLIN' STOPPED AND THEY ALL TOOK A
 DRINK
TO THE HEALTH OF OL' CURLY JOE.

HE DRANK TO CONTENT, AND THEN OVER HE WENT
TO THE TABLE THAT HAD THE MOST DOUGH.

NOW HE RESTED HIS ARMS ON A TABLE OF GREEN
AND ASKED FOR A PASSEL OF DRAW.
THEY DEALT HIM A DEUCE, A TREY AND A QUEEN,
THE WORST HAND THAT HE'D EVER SAW.
THEN CAME TWO MORE CARDS, A 4 AND A 5,
THAT LEFT HIM NEEDING A 6.
BUT THEY DEALT HIM AN 8, AND THAT RUINED HIS
    STRAIGHT,
THEN HE KNEW THEY WERE UP TO THEIR TRICKS.

NOW HE ASKED FOR THE DEAL AND HE PICKED UP THE
    CARDS
AND R-R-R-RIP! THEY FELL IN THEIR PLACES.
AND THEN FROM THE MIDDLE, THE BOTTOM AND TOP
HE DEALT OFF THOSE 4 LITTLE ACES.
NOW HE KNEW IN A GLANCE HE WAS A-BETTIN' HIS
    PANTS
SO THE DOUGH HE LAID ON THE LINE.
HE SAID, IF YOU PLEASE, I'LL JUST PLAY THESE,
I THINK THIS HANDS A-MIGHTY FINE.

NOW THEY PLACED THEIR BETS AND SPREAD THEIR
    CARDS
UPON THE TABLE OF GREEN.
THEN OL' CURLY JOE RAKED IN THE DOUGH,
4 ACES WAS OVER 4 QUEENS.
THEN A SHOT RANG OUT IN OL' BOOTHEEL SALOON,
POOR CURLY FELL TO THE FLOOR.
HE WHISPERED AND SIGHED, SOMEBODY HAS LIED,
4 ACES DON'T WIN ANY MO-O-O-ORE.

   ALL.
CURLY JOE FROM IDAHO, A RAMBLIN' GAMBLIN' ROVER,
HE DEALT FROM THE BOTTOM, HE DEALT FROM THE TOP,
BUT NOW HIS DEALING IS OVER.

(APPLAUSE LIGHT.
LESLIE takes swig from bottle, returns to chair US.
ARCHIE joins MILES, CLIVE and MABEL at C mike with script.)

ARCHIE. Well, Aces, it's Christmas, and 'ere we are in jolly old England.
MILES. Yeah, so what?
CLIVE. Aces! That's no way to talk. At this season of the year, everybody's happy.
MILES. Hmmph.
MABEL. Everybody's on their best behavior.
ACES. I was on my best behavior last year, and what did I get? Nothing.
MABEL. Nothing? Well, surely your good friend Jack gave you something.
MILES. Ha! Jack is so stingy, as soon as December rolls around he starts dreaming of a tight Christmas.
ARCHIE. Aces, I'm surprised at you. A cowboy never thinks about what 'e's going to get — but what 'e's going to give.

(ARCHIE strums intro chords on his guitar.)

MUSIC INTRO: "CHRISTMAS ON THE RANGE"

(ARCHIE and MILES sit side by side, as if riding a wagon. CLIVE stands behind and in between them.)

ARCHIE.
WHEN IT'S CHRISTMAS ON THE RANGE
AND THE HILLS ARE SNOWY WHITE,
COME HOME, COWBOY, COME HOME.

WHEN IT'S CHRISTMAS ON THE RANGE
AND MY LONELY HEART IS LIGHT,
COME HOME, COWBOY, TONIGHT.

ARCHIE, MILES & CLIVE.
GOT MY HORSE A SADDLE,

> ARCHIE.
> BROTHER JOE A HAT.
>
> ARCHIE, MILES & CLIVE.
> GOT MY MA A DRESS OF GINGHAM
> AND A LITTLE BIT OF THIS AND THAT.
> GOT MY SIS A LOCKET,
>
> ARCHIE.
> DAD'LL DO ALL RIGHT.
> NOT A PENNY IN MY POCKET,
>
> ARCHIE, MILES & CLIVE.
> BUT I'M HAPPY RIDIN' HOME TONIGHT.
>
> ARCHIE.
> THERE'S A GIRL DOWN AT THE GRANGE
> AND I'M BRINGING HER MY HEART,
> WHEN IT'S CHRISTMAS ON THE RANGE.
>
> ARCHIE, MILES & CLIVE.
> GOT MY HORSE A SADDLE,
>
> ARCHIE.
> BROTHER JOE A HAT.
>
> ARCHIE, MILES & CLIVE.
> GOT MY MA A DRESS OF GINGHAM
> AND A LITTLE BIT OF THIS AND THAT.
> GOT MY SIS A LOCKET,
>
> ARCHIE.
> DAD'LL DO ALL RIGHT.
> NOT A PENNY IN MY POCKET,
>
> ARCHIE, MILES & CLIVE.
> BUT I'M HAPPY RIDIN' HOME TONIGHT.

ARCHIE.
THERE'S A GIRL DOWN AT THE GRANGE
AND I'M BRINGING HER MY HEART,
WHEN IT'S CHRISTMAS ON THE RANGE.

(During the repeat, MABEL gets into the Christmas spirit. She picks up CLIVE's box of presents from beneath the tree, and passes out gifts to the boys. LESLIE winds up with the bottle of whiskey. He gladly takes a deep swig, returns to chair US. APPLAUSE LIGHT.)

    ARCHIE. Come on, boys, let's hit the trail.
    MILES. I'm right behind you!

(ARCHIE walks to SR mike, followed by MILES, who is completely unaware that the "dummy" is not supposed to be able to walk. ALL stare at MILES.)

    MABEL. *(Covers her mike, stage whisper.)* Aces, wait! You can't walk.
    MILES. *(Freezes)* I can't?
    MABEL. *(Hissing)* No, you can't. You're the dummy. Remember?
    MILES. *(Into mike, covering.)* That's right... I am... But uh, uh, um... through the magic of radio I've been... I've been.... *(Honk!)*
    CLIVE. You've been honked?
    ARCHIE. *(Aside to MABEL.)* He's panicking!
    MILES. *(Honk!)*
    MABEL. *(Aside)* Do something, Jack.
    MILES. *(Honk!)*
    CLIVE. *(Thinking on his feet.)* Aces! You've been transformed! It's a Christmas miracle! Look, everybody! Aces has turned into a real boy! *(Holds arms out to MILES.)* Pinocchio!

    MILES. *(Confused but covering.)* Father?

(LESLIE lurches forward. He's pretty bombed by now and completely drops the charade. MABEL covers mike with hand.)

LESLIE. This is absurd. They know you can walk. They saw you in the intro. They're not stupid. *(Looks out at house.)* Are you?
ARCHIE. Leslie!
LESLIE. The bloomin' idiot sang a duet with him!
MILES. What was I supposed to do? It said duet right there on the page. Un. Doo. Ette.

(The warning tones sound. Without skipping a beat LESLIE turns to nearest mike, takes script handed to him by STAN and reads. The words are sobering.)

LESLIE. This special holiday programme is coming to you live from the BBC, and is being broadcast even as we speak to the millions of allied troops now fighting for freedom and democracy in the foxholes of France, the fields of Belgium and Holland, and the hills of Italy. From every one of us here at Broadcasting House in London— *(Looks at the rest of the cast.)* — and I do mean, everyone — we want you lads to know that we're pulling for you. We wish you Godspeed, and good fortune.
ARCHIE. Thank you, Les, er, Slappy. *(To ALL.)* Shall we get on with the show?

(ALL nod. As ARCHIE picks up the scene from the radio script, CLIVE and MILES join him at DR mike. LESLIE EXITS.)

ARCHIE. So — here we are on the trail, with our horses tucked all snug in their beds, and our cattle pals settling down for a nice prairie nap.

(SFX: Wind. Campfire.)

MILES. Brrrrr, but it's cold out here on the trail.
CLIVE. Move closer to the campfire, Aces.

MILES. If I move any closer, Jack, I'll *be* the campfire.

(SFX: Coyote howl.)

MILES. Yikes! What was that?

ARCHIE. That was the coyote's mating call.
MILES. Mating call? Sure sounds like they hate to get married.

(MABEL sings yodeling start of CATTLE CALL at SL mike.)

MILES. Now you can't tell me *that* was a coyote's mating call.
CLIVE. No, it sounded more like Mabel's cattle call. Looks like she's joined us on our trail ride.
MILES. It's getting awfully crowded on the lonesome trail.
CLIVE. I like the company.
MILES. Yeah, it's always nice to meet a fellow cow pusher.
CLIVE. Puncher.
MILES. Beg your pardon?
CLIVE. *(Points to script.)* Puncher.
MILES. I'd rather kiss her. But if you insist.

(MILES winds up; CLIVE stops him.)

ARCHIE. Now cut that out! You two settle down nice-like and listen to what Miss Mabel has to say.

(MABEL steps up to SC mike as band plays:)

MUSIC INTRO: "CATTLE CALL"

MABEL.
THE CATTLE ARE PROWLIN',
THE COYOTES ARE HOWLIN',
WAY OUT WHERE THE DOGIES BAWL.
WHERE SPURS ARE A-JINGLIN',
THE COWBOY IS SINGIN',
THIS LONESOME CATTLE CALL.

DO-WHOO-OO, etc.

MABEL & MILES.
HE RIDES IN THE SUN
TIL HIS DAY'S WORK IS DONE

AND HE ROUNDS UP THE CATTLE EACH FALL.

DOO-WHOO, etc.
SINGIN' HIS CATTLE CALL.

    MABEL.
FOR HOURS HE WOULD RIDE
O'ER THE RANGE FAR AND WIDE,
AS THE NIGHT WINDS BLOW UP A SQUALL,
HIS HEART'S LIKE A FEATHER
IN ALL KINDS OF WEATHER
AS HE SINGS HIS CATTLE CALL.

    MABEL, MILES & CLIVE.
DOO-WHOO, etc.
HE'S BROWN AS A BERRY
FROM RIDIN' THE PRAIRIE
AND HE SINGS WITH AN OLD WESTERN DRAWL.

DOO-WHOO, ETC.
SINGIN' HIS CATTLE CALL.

(APPLAUSE LIGHT)

    MILES. *(On script.)* The life of a cowboy seems kinda lonesome.
    ARCHIE. *(On script.)* It ain't so bad. I mean, just look at the stars up above. Millions of tiny little lights shining down on us. And in the daytime, there's cows — *(SFX: Cow moo, cowbell. ALL do slow take to STAN, who shrugs.)* And tumbleweeds.

(SFX: Wind.)

    MUSIC INTRO: "*TUMBLIN' TUMBLEWEEDS*"

    ARCHIE.
I'M A ROVING COWBOY RIDIN' ALL DAY LONG
TUMBLEWEEDS AROUND ME HEAR MY LONELY SONG
NIGHTS UNDERNEATH A PRAIRIE MOON

I RIDE ALONE AND SING A TUNE.

ALL.
SEE THEM TUMBLIN' DOWN,
PLEDGING THEIR LOVE TO THE GROUND,
LONELY BUT FREE I'LL BE FOUND,
DRIFTIN' ALONG WITH THE TUMBLIN' TUMBLEWEEDS.

CARES OF THE PAST ARE BEHIND,
NOWHERE TO GO BUT I'LL FIND
JUST WHERE THE TRAIL WILL WIND,
DRIFTIN' ALONG WITH THE TUMBLIN' TUMBLEWEEDS.

ARCHIE.
I KNOW WHEN NIGHT IS GONE
THAT A NEW WORLD'S BORN AT DAWN.

ALL.
I'LL KEEP ROLLING ALONG,
DEEP IN MY HEART IS A SONG,
HERE ON THE RANGE I BELONG,
DRIFTIN' ALONG WITH THE TUMBLIN' TUMBLEWEEDS.

ARCHIE. (ENSEMBLE)
I KNOW (I KNOW)
WHEN NIGHT IS GONE (NIGHT IS GONE)
THAT A NEW WORLD'S BORN AT DAWN.

ALL.
I'LL KEEP ROLLING ALONG,
DEEP IN MY HEART IS A SONG,
HERE ON THE RANGE I BELONG,
DRIFTIN' ALONG WITH THE TUMBLIN' TUMBLEWEEDS.

(APPLAUSE LIGHT.)

ARCHIE. *(On script; others join him at his mike.)* All right, boys. It's time to hit the hay. We've got a long day tomorrow.

MILES. *(Drowsily)* I'm so sleepy...good ol' sleeping bag. Ah, this is the life for me... G'night, everybody.

(ALL snore twice; SFX: alarm clock rings.)

ARCHIE. Wake up, Aces. It's 3 o'clock.
MILES. Wha — what happened to the night?
ARCHIE. Rides start early on the trail.
MILES. Who's the trail boss, an owl?
ARCHIE. We've got a lot of cows to move today.
MILES. Yeah, well, do we have to sneak up on 'em in the dark?
ARCHIE. Dark? Why, that's daylight coming through over yonder.
MILES. Well, let's crawl back in the sack before the darn stuff gets all over us.

(LESLIE bursts in USL door, twanging a dinner triangle. He's in white apron, chef's hat with sprig of holly, a wooden spoon in one hand — and completely snockered.)

LESLIE. *(Bellows)* Come and get it — whoaahhhhhh!

(LESLIE loses balance and falls backward out the door.)

CLIVE. If it isn't old Slappy Burdette!

(LESLIE bounces back in through door and strikes jaunty pose.)

CLIVE. Looking rather jolly. What's he doing on this cattle drive?
ARCHIE. He's the chuck wagon cook.
MILES. Shoot me now!

(LESLIE goes to C mike as band plays:)

MUSIC INTRO: *"COME 'N' GET IT"*

LESLIE.
COME 'N GET IT!

ARCHIE.
COME 'N GET IT!

CLIVE.
COME 'N GET IT!

MILES.
COME 'N GET IT!

MABEL.
COME 'N GET IT!

LESLIE. (ALL)
NOW ALL YOU FOLKS SHOULD SING WITH GLEE
(OH YES, OH YES)
TO HAVE A MARV'LOUS COOK LIKE ME.
(AIN'T IT SO, AIN'T IT SO)
FROM O-RAY-GON TO THE TEXAS PLAIN,
I'VE COOKED ON BOATS AND CATTLE TRAINS.
I'LL COOK YOU ANYTHING YOU WISH
BUT PINTO BEANS IS MY FAVO-RITE DISH.
(HE'LL COOK YOU ANYTHING YOU WISH
BUT PINTO BEANS IS HIS FAVO-RITE DISH)

ALL.
BEANS FOR BREAKFAST, BEANS FOR DINNER,
BEANS FOR SUPPER, LORD, DELIVER US FROM THAT.

LESLIE.
I'LL TAKE A BONE AND A CACTUS ROOT,
(OH YES, OH YES)
A HUNK OF TOWEL AND AN OL' BROWN BOOT,
(AIN'T IT SO, AIN'T IT SO)
THEN I'LL PUT HER ON AND I'LL BOIL HER DOWN,
TILL THE FLOOR CURLS UP AND THE AIR TURNS BROWN.
BUT SAY YOUR PRAYERS AND KNOCK ON WOOD
'CAUSE YOU MAY DIE SOONER THAN YOU THOUGHT
    YOU WOULD.
(WE'LL SAY OUR PRAYERS AND KNOCK ON WOOD

'CAUSE WE MAY DIE SOONER THAN WE THOUGHT WE
WOULD.)

ALL.
HASH FOR BREAKFAST, HASH FOR DINNER,
HASH FOR SUPPER, LORD, DELIVER US FROM THAT.

LESLIE.
WHEN ALL MY WORK ON EARTH IS THROUGH,
(OH YES, OH YES)
I'LL GO AND JOIN THAT HEAVENLY CREW
(AIN'T IT SO, AIN'T IT SO)
I'LL TELL ST. PETER AT THE PEARLY WHITE GATES
I'M THE BEST DURN COOK IN THE 48 STATES
WITH MY CORNPONE PATTIES AND ROASTIN' EARS
I'LL KEEP 'EM HAPPY FOR A MILLION YEARS.
(WITH HIS CORNPONE PATTIES AND HIS ROASTIN' EARS
HE'LL KEEP 'EM HAPPY FOR A MILLION YEARS.)

ALL.
CORN FOR BREAKFAST, CORN FOR DINNER,
CORN FOR SUPPER, LORD, DELIVER US FROM THAT.

LESLIE.
AIN'T IT SO!

MABEL.
AIN'T IT SO!

MILES.
AIN'T IT SO!

ARCHIE.
AIN'T IT SO!

CLIVE.
AIN'T IT SO!

(APPLAUSE LIGHT.
CLIVE & MILES join LESLIE at C with script. MABEL and ARCHIE stay DR, with scripts.
SFX: "Spee-ow!" ricochet sound, ALL duck.)

LESLIE. *(Reads script.)* I say, chaps, we're being surrounded by bad guys.

(SFX: "Spee-ow!" ricochet off a tin plate.)

MILES. YEOOWWWW!
CLIVE. What's the matter, Aces?
MILES. He shot a bullet in the air, he punctured me, I can't say where.
CLIVE. Are you really hit?
MILES. Yeah, he got me right in the knothole.
MABEL. Stand back, I'll scare 'em with this.

(SFX: series of gun shots.)

CLIVE. Now hold on there, Miss Mabel. That ain't no way to treat a bad guy.
MABEL. It ain't?
CLIVE. No. These days you have to use psychology. It used to be the really rotten ones were driven by the grossest possible goals. Money. Women. Now there's no such thing as a bad cowpoke. Only a sick one...

(MABEL EXITS to change as CHAPS take positions around C mike.)

MUSIC INTRO: "GUNSLINGER"

CLIVE.
GUNSLINGER!

ARCHIE.
GUNSLINGER!

LESLIE.
GUNSLINGER!

MILES.
GUNSLINGER!

ALL.
GUNSLINGER, GUNSLINGER, WHERE DID YOU GO WRONG?
WHEN YOU WERE A CHILD, DID THE CHEYENNE AND SIOUX
REFUSE TO PLAY NICELY WITH YOU?
DID YOU ALWAYS FEEL YOU DIDN'T BELONG?
GUNSLINGER!

CLIVE. (ALL)
YOU KILLED 130 MEN, OLD BUDDY
(GUNSLINGER! GUNSLINGER!)
(AND NOW YOU WANT TO SETTLE DOWN.
BUT OTHER GUNSLINGERS ARE A-GUNNIN' FOR YOU)

CLIVE.
AND A MAN'S GOTTA DO WHAT A MAN'S GOTTA DO

ALL.
OLD BUDDY!

GUNSLINGER, GUNSLINGER, WHY YOU ACT SO STRANGE?

CLIVE.
WHEN YOU WERE A CHILD WERE YOU FORCED TO COMPETE
WITH BROTHERS THAT YOU NEVER COULD BEAT
DID YOU COME FROM A BROKEN

ALL.
HOME ON THE RANGE? OLD BUDDY!

CLIVE.
DON'T WEAR YOUR GUNS IN TOWN TODAY, OLD BUDDY.

ALL.
LAST NIGHT YOU CRIED OUT MOMMIE DEAR.

CLIVE.
YOU'VE GOT A RECURRENT DREAM IN YOUR CRAW AND THAT DREAM OF YOUR MA WILL INHIBIT YOUR DRAW.

CLIVE.
OLD BUDDY!

ARCHIE.
OLD BUDDY!

LESLIE.
OLD BUDDY!

MILES.
OLD BUDDY!

ALL.
YIPPEE-I-AY! YIPPEE-I-OH!
GUNSLINGER, GUNSLINGER, PLEASE TAKE MY ADVICE.

ARCHIE. You know in your mind that you're plumb insecure.
LESLIE. And that killin' a man is real immature.
CLIVE. It's just an attention getting —

ALL.
DE-VICE! GUNSLINGER!

MILES.
THERE YOU LIE, DEAD IN THE DUST, OL' BUDDY.

ALL. Ol' buddy.

AND NOW YOUR MYTH BEGINS.

CLIVE.
OUT IN THE WEST THE FOLKS ALL BELIEVE

ALL.
YOU FACED AND KILLED THE TOUGHEST
HOMBRES OF YOUR DAY.
BUT TIME HAS EXPOSED YOUR FEET OF CLAY.

CLIVE. Recent research has clearly shown that 93.6 percent of the gunmen you killed —

ALL.
WERE SIMPLY ACCIDENT PRONE! GUNSLINGER!

(APPLAUSE LIGHT.
CHAPS at C mike. During the next sketch, they fix their focus on a point at the back of the theatre. As the "cattle" draw closer, their bodies gradually shake and tremble, as though the ground was shaking beneath them, building to a crescendo.
SFX: "MOOOOOOOOOOOO!" through bull horn.)

MILES. *(On script.)* I don't want to frighten anybody. But there's a great big crowd of cows coming this way.
ARCHIE. No need to panic, chaps. That's our 'erd of cattle. They're simply excited. And well they should be, first day out on the trail and all. I'd say they're just itchin' to start the drive.

(SFX: thunder sheet, starts easy, builds to a roar.)

MILES. That's some itch.
LESLIE. Yes, only a mosquito of giant proportions could cause that kind of scratching. Look at them run.
MILES. How fast would you say they're going?
LESLIE. Taking into consideration the refraction of the light, the angle of that ravine and wind factor, I'd say they were doing about 40 knots.

CLIVE. 40 knots! That's rather speedy. How many of them would you say there were? Five? Six hundred?
LESLIE. Oh, my word, no. There have to be at least a thousand, maybe two.
MILES. Two thousand cattle running full tilt this way.
ALL. *(Musing)* Yes...
MILES. This isn't a cattle drive — it's a bloomin' stampede!
LESLIE. What do we do now?

(MABEL ENTERS resplendent in Act Two spangly cowgirl costume, goes to SR mike and whistles; CHAPS stop shaking, thundersheet stops.)

MABEL. The only thing we can do — SING!

(ALL whistle and "yee-haw" to mike positions for:)

MUSIC INTRO: *"RIDE, COWBOY, RIDE"*

MABEL.
UP IN THE MORNING AT THE BREAK OF DAY

MILES.
YOU'LL HEAR A BIG-BEARDED COWBOY
AT THE CHUCKWAGON SAY

CLIVE.
GATHER ROUND, BOYS, THE COFFEE'S HOT ON THE FIRE
THERE'S A FULL DAY OF BRANDIN', WE'RE HEATIN' THE IRON.

ARCHIE.
I WANT TO SMELL THAT SCORCHED HAIR AND BURNIN' HIDE,
THE HORSE ARE REINED, BOYS, THEY'RE READY TO RIDE.

LESLIE.
ROLL UP YOUR BED ROLLS AND JUMP IN YOUR BOOTS

ALL.
DAYLIGHT IS A-WASTIN, BOYS, IT'S OUT OF THE CHUTE.

COME ON AND RIDE, COWBOY, RIDE!
ROLL UP YOUR REATAS,
AND PULL YOUR SOMBREROS DOWN TIGHT.
WE'RE GOING TO RIDE, RIDE, RIDE,
WHERE THE TRAIL WILL WIND
YOU BETTER DRIVE, DRIVE, DRIVE
OR WE'LL LEAVE YOU BEHIND.
COME ON AND RIDE — RIDE — RIDE — COWBOY, RIDE!

MILES.
IT'S A BEAUTIFUL MORNIN' AND YOU'VE HAD A GOOD REST.
YOU ROPERS, GET READY TO BE AT YOUR BEST

CLIVE.
LET'S SADDLE THEM PONIES AND TIGHTEN THE CINCH.
PULL ON YOUR GLOVES AND TAKE YOUR HAT OFF THE FENCE.

ARCHIE.
WE'LL GET THE CATTLE TO MARKET AND AFTER THEY'RE SOLD,
YOU CAN ALL LET YER HAIR DOWN, GET LAZY OR BOLD.

MABEL.
RIDE INTO TOWN AND FIND A LADY OR TWO

ALL.
TO TAKE YOU BY THE ARMS
AND SHAKE THAT DUST OFF YOUR BOOTS.
COME AND RIDE, COWBOY, RIDE.
ROLL UP YOUR REATAS AND PULL YOUR SOMBREROS DOWN TIGHT.
WE'RE GOING TO RIDE, RIDE, RIDE,
WHERE THE TRAIL WILL WIND.
YOU BETTER DRIVE, DRIVE, DRIVE

OR WE'LL LEAVE YOU BEHIND.
COME ON AND RIDE — RIDE — RIDE — COWBOY, RIDE!

(As the COWBOYS & MABEL hit the finale, the air raid siren creeps in on the same note. It takes a moment before anyone notices.)

O.S. WOMAN'S VOICE FROM BOOTH. Air raid, everybody! The alert has sounded. Please, take cover in the lobby. Air raid!

LESLIE. Thank heavens. Now we can rehearse!

BLACK OUT

ACT II

(At five minutes, "All Clear" siren sounds in black out. PA announces to audience in lobby: All clear! All clear! You may return to your seats. All clear!"
When lights come up, band is in place. CAST ENTER in what appear to be the same costumes as end of Act I, take positions at mikes. They're pumped up, ready to go, in control at last.)

ARCHIE. *(Counting off.)* A-one, two, a-one, two, three —

(CAST and BAND kick into opening bars of RAGTIME COWBOY JOE. Almost immediately, huge explosion is heard. Lights flicker in strobe effect as the CAST careen back and forth as if being blown about. Blackout. The sound of the explosion continues as in the dark the CAST rip off tearaway costume pieces, toss them behind the bandstand. The set is rigged to self-destruct. House lights come to half, with green stage "work" lights. It's clear the studio has been hit. Ceiling debris is scattered across the floor. Microphones are tipped over, chairs, stools and tables knocked down on their sides including the SFX table [STAN is hidden behind it] but this should be finessed to make it easy to reset. The big logo over the bandstand is hanging by one corner, pictures and posters are askew or dangling.)

ARCHIE. *(Carries guitar.)* Is — is everyone all right?
MABEL. I'm not sure.

LESLIE. Neither am I.
ARCHIE. *(Looks to back of house or balcony.)* How about you up there? Thumbs up!
CLIVE. Well, that gave me a bit of a fright, I must say.
MILES. It appears the Beeb's taken a direct hit.
MABEL. For a second there I thought we'd bought the farm.
LESLIE. Talk about bringing the house down.
ARCHIE. The generators must be out. But I'm sure the lads will 'ave the power back on in half a mo'.
MILES. *(Remembers)* Stan? Are you there?

(STAN rises up from beneath the SFX table, toots horn. They shake hands.)

MILES. We're all right, then.
ALL. Yes. I believe so. I think I am.
ARCHIE. *(To studio audience.)* So...'ere we are, and there you are, and — well, we 'ave no power, no radio and no broadcast. *(Beat)* You know, when that bomb was whistlin' over our heads, I could've lost 'eart. But I didn't. I kept thinking of a time when this terrible mess would be over, and we'd all be sitting around the fire with our loved ones again, enjoying a nice cup of Christmas cheer —
CLIVE. And a delicious packet of Saltey's Fish 'N Chips. "Puts a smile on your face —"
LESLIE. Oh, Clive, really!
CLIVE. Well, believe it or not, I *like* the blasted things.
ARCHIE. But you know what I'm trying to say. Don'cher?
MABEL. I think I do.

MUSIC INTRO:
"WHITE CLIFFS OF DOVER/I'LL BE HOME FOR CHRISTMAS"

(MABEL sings á capella. After a line ARCHIE starts to chord along on the guitar.)

MABEL.
THERE'LL BE BLUEBIRDS OVER THE WHITE CLIFFS OF DOVER
TOMORROW, JUST YOU WAIT AND SEE.

THERE'LL BE LOVE AND LAUGHTER AND PEACE EVER
   AFTER
TOMORROW WHEN THE WORLD IS FREE.

THE SHEPHERD WILL TEND HIS SHEEP,
THE VALLEY WILL BLOOM AGAIN.
AND JIMMY WILL GO TO SLEEP
IN HIS OWN LITTLE ROOM AGAIN.

   ARCHIE.
I'LL BE HOME FOR CHRISTMAS
YOU CAN COUNT ON ME.

   CLIVE.
PLEASE HAVE SNOW, AND MISTLETOE

   LESLIE.
AND PRESENTS 'ROUND THE TREE.

   MILES.
CHRISTMAS EVE WILL FIND ME
WHERE THE LOVE LIGHT GLEAMS,

   BOYS.
I'LL BE HOME FOR CHRISTMAS
IF ONLY IN MY DREAMS.

   MABEL & MILES.
THE SHEPHERD WILL TEND HIS SHEEP,
THE VALLEY WILL BLOOM AGAIN.
AND JIMMY WILL GO TO SLEEP
IN HIS OWN LITTLE ROOM AGAIN.

   MABEL. (BOYS)
THERE'LL BE BLUEBIRDS OVER
THE WHITE CLIFFS OF DOVER
(CHRISTMAS EVE WILL FIND ME
WHERE THE LOVE LIGHT GLEAMS.
I'LL BE HOME FOR CHRISTMAS)

TOMORROW — JUST YOU WAIT AND SEE.
(IF ONLY IN MY DREAMS.)

(Stage lights flicker back on abruptly.)

    ARCHIE. That's it, then!
    MILES. I don't believe it. We have power.
    O.S. WOMAN'S VOICE IN BOOTH. And we're back on the air!
    MILES. *What?*
    CLIVE. On the air!
    MILES. Good heavens! What do we do?
    ARCHIE. I s'pose we just carry on!
    LESLIE. *(Gestures to burnt-up costume.)* Like this? Good lord.
    CLIVE. And my script's exploded.
    MABEL. Listen, boys, the troops are counting on us. We can't let them down.
    ARCHIE. *(Puts arm around MABEL.)* I'm with Mabel.
    MABEL. *(A special smile for ARCHIE.)* Thanks, Archie. I'm with you, too.

SFX: "On The Air" chimes.
CLIVE pushes LESLIE to the microphone, as he IS the BBC announcer.)

    LESLIE. *(With golden tones.)* This is Tex Riley's Radio Round-up. And...*(Turns to MILES for help.)*
    MILES. *(Steps up to the mike.)* We apologize for that unscheduled interruption.
    CLIVE. *(Joins MILES.)* It seems a few nasty visitors paid us a call.
    ARCHIE. *(Joins CLIVE & MILES.)* But we want you lads at the front to know it's going to take more than a bomb from old Jerry to shut us up!
    ALL. *(General ad lib.)* Right you are! Yes, indeed! You can say that again, etc.

(MABEL and the BOYS scramble to pick up script pages.)

ARCHIE. And, um, while we're pulling ourselves together...
MABEL. *(Pops up at mike.)* Let's hear a little number from the band. C'mon, boys — swing it!

(The BAND breaks into an up-tempo instrumental [fiddler's choice] which lasts long enough for the cast to EXIT and make a quick change. At the end of number:
APPLAUSE LIGHT.
During applause, CAST RE-ENTERS in spiffy cowboy gear and chaps. ARCHIE counts them in, and they hum RAGTIME COWBOY JOE under MABEL's intro.)

MUSIC INTRO: "RAGTIME COWBOY JOE"

(Staging of the Cowboy Joe adventure segment should be highly stylized. The actors should mime the sfx, like opening doors, riding horses, drawing guns, etc. The sketch works best when the characters [Sue, Joe, etc.] are played "straight" and earnest, not melodrama-hokey — just like the old radio shows.)

MABEL. Join us now as we return to those singin', swingin' days of the old West. Yes, folks — it's time for an exciting Christmas adventure with Cowboy Joe and his Lonesome Rangers.

ALL.
HE ALWAYS SINGS
RAGGY MUSIC TO THE CATTLE AS HE SWINGS
BACK AND FORWARD IN THE SADDLE ON A HORSE
THAT IS SYNCOPATED GAITED
AND IT'S SUCH A FUNNY METER
TO THE ROAR OF HIS REPEATER.

HOW THEY RUN
WHEN THEY HEAR THE FELLA'S GUN
BECAUSE THE WESTERN FOLKS ALL KNOW,
HE'S A HIGH-FALUTIN', ROOTIN' TOOTIN'
SON-OF-A-GUN FROM ARIZONA,
RAGTIME COWBOY JOE.

OUT IN ARIZONA WHERE THE BAD MEN ARE
THE ONLY THING TO GUIDE YOU IS AN EVENING STAR.
ROUGHEST TOUGHEST MAN BY FAR
IS RAGTIME COWBOY JOE.

GOT HIS NAME FROM SINGING TO THE COWS AND SHEEP.
EVERY NIGHT THEY SAY HE SANG THE HERD TO SLEEP,
IN A BASS SO RICH AND DEEP
CROONIN' SOFT AND LOW.

HE ALWAYS SINGS
RAGGY MUSIC TO THE CATTLE AS HE SWINGS
BACK AND FORWARD IN THE SADDLE ON A HORSE
THAT IS SYNCOPATED GAITED
AND IT'S SUCH A FUNNY METER
TO THE ROAR OF HIS REPEATER.

HOW THEY RUN
WHEN THEY HEAR THE FELLA'S GUN
BECAUSE THE WESTERN FOLKS ALL KNOW,
HE'S A HIGH-FALUTIN', ROOTIN' TOOTIN'
SON-OF-A-GUN FROM ARIZONA,
RAGTIME COWBOY JOE.

    ALL.
COWBOY!

(MABEL points to ARCHIE.)

    ARCHIE. That's me!?

    ALL
COWBOY!

    ARCHIE. That's me!

    ALL.
RAGTIME COWBOY JOE!

CHAPS! A JINGLE JANGLE CHRISTMAS

(APPLAUSE LIGHT.
The BOYS start a finger-poppin' rhythm for COOL WATER during MABEL's speech, making a "flying V" formation with ARCHIE at the point.)

MABEL. Cowboy Joe and his Lonesome Rangers have been riding across the desert for days now, hot on the trail of the Pecos Kid — wanted dead or alive for telling children there ain't no Santy Claus. Their throats are raw, their canteens nearly dry, but still they ride on.
CLIVE. I say, Joe, we been wanderin' around this blasted wasteland for days and not a drop of water in sight.
ARCHIE. Be patient, boys, it's out here somewhere. I know we'll find it. But while we're looking, why don't you saddle pals join me in a song?

MUSIC INTRO: *"COOL WATER: á capella."*

ARCHIE.
ALL DAY I'VE FACED THE BARREN WASTE
WITHOUT A TASTE OF WATER.

ALL. (MABEL in parentheses)
COOL WATER (WATER)

ARCHIE. (MABEL)
OL' DAN AND I WITH THROATS BURNED DRY
AND SOULS THAT CRY FOR WATER. (WATER)

ALL. (MABEL)
COOL (WATER) CLEAR (WATER) WATER (WATER WATER)

KEEP A-MOVING, DAN, (WATER)
DON'T YOU LISTEN TO HIM, DAN. (WATER)
HE'S A DEVIL, NOT A MAN (WATER)
WHEN HE SPREADS THE BURNING SANDS (WATER)
WITH WATER. (WATER, WATER)
DAN, CAN YOU SEE (WATER)
THAT BIG GREEN TREE (WATER)

WHERE THE WATER'S RUNNIN' FREE (WATER)
AND IT'S WAITIN' THERE FOR ME (WATER)
AND YOU? (COOL, CLEAR WATER)

ARCHIE.
THE SHADOWS SWAY AND SEEM TO SAY
TONIGHT WE PRAY FOR WATER.

ALL. (MABEL)
COOL WATER. (WATER)

ARCHIE. (MABEL)
AND WAY UP THERE HE'LL HEAR OUR PRAYER
AND SHOW US WHERE THERE'S WATER. (WATER)

ALL. (MABEL)
COOL (WATER) CLEAR (WATER) WATER. (WATER, WATER)

KEEP A-MOVING, DAN. (WATER)
DON'T YOU LISTEN TO HIM, DAN. (WATER)
HE'S A DEVIL, NOT A MAN (WATER)
WHEN HE SPREADS THE BURNING SANDS (WATER)
WITH WATER. (WATER, WATER)
DAN, CAN YOU SEE (WATER)
THAT BIG GREEN TREE (WATER)
WHERE THE WATER'S RUNNIN' FREE (WATER)
AND IT'S WAITIN' THERE FOR ME(WATER)
AND YOU? (COOL, CLEAR WATER)

COOL (WATER) CLEAR (WATER) WATER. (WATER, WATER)
COOL (WATER) CLEAR (WATER)

MABEL.
COOL, CLEAR WATER!

(SFX: thunder crash, rain.)

ARCHIE. Ask and you shall receive. Grab yer canteens and fill 'em up.

BOYS. Yee-haw!

(SFX: Train whistle. MABEL waves as if she's just arrived on a train. ALL use scripts.)

    MABEL. Hey cowboys! Yoo-hoo, fellers!
    CLIVE. Why, look, it's our old gal Sue.
    MILES. Ah yes, dear old Saratoga Sue.
    CLIVE. No, *this* Sue has eyes of blue.
    MILES. Blue?
    CLIVE. Blue.
    MILES. From Sasketoo?
    CLIVE. No, not that Sue.
    MILES. From Kalamazoo?
    CLIVE. Look, why don't I sing it for you?
    LESLIE. Do.

        MUSIC INTRO: *"SIOUX CITY SUE"*

CLIVE.
WE DROVE A HERD OF CATTLE DOWN
FROM OLD NEBRASKEE WAY

    MILES.
THAT'S HOW WE COME TO BE IN THE STATE OF IOWAY.

    CLIVE.
I MET A GAL IN IOWAY.

    MILES.
THAT'S FUNNY, I DID, TOO.

    CLIVE.
I ASKED HER WHAT HER NAME WAS, SHE SAID

    MABEL.
SIOUX CITY SUE.

    CLIVE.
SIOUX CITY SUE.

MILES.
SIOUX CITY SUE.

CLIVE.
HER HAIR IS BLONDE.

MILES.
HER EYES ARE BLUE.

CLIVE.
I SWAPPED MY HORSE—

MILES.
MY DOG FOR SUE.

ALL.
SIOUX CITY SUE, SIOUX CITY SUE.
THERE AIN'T NO GAL AS TRUE AS MY SWEET SIOUX CITY SUE.

MILES.
I ASKED HER IF SHE HAD A BEAU, SHE SAID

MABEL.
YES, QUITE A FEW.

MILES.
BUT STILL I STARTED COURTING MY SWEET SIOUX CITY SUE.

CLIVE.
THE FIRST TIME THAT I STOLE A KISS
I CAUGHT HER STEALIN' TWO.
I ASKED HER, DID SHE LOVE ME? SHE SAID

MABEL.
INDEED I DO.

MILES & CLIVE.
SIOUX CITY SUE, SIOUX CITY SUE.
YOUR HAIR IS BLONDE, YOUR EYES ARE BLUE.
I'D SWAP MY HORSE AND DOG FOR YOU.
SIOUX CITY SUE, SIOUX CITY SUE.
THERE AIN'T NO GAL AS TRUE AS MY SWEET SIOUX CITY SUE.

CLIVE.
NOW WE'RE ADMITTIN', IOWAY, WE OWE A LOT TO YOU.

MILES.
CAUSE WE COME FROM NEBRASKEE TO FIND SIOUX CITY SUE.

MILES. *(In cahoots with CLIVE.)*
I'M GONNA ROPE AND TIE HER UP.

CLIVE.
WE'LL USE MY OL' LASSOO!

MILES.
WE'RE GONNA PUT OUR BRAND ON MY SWEET SIOUX CITY SUE.

ALL.
SIOUX CITY SUE, SIOUX CITY SUE.
YOUR HAIR IS BLONDE YOUR EYES ARE BLUE.
I'D SWAP MY HORSE AND DOG FOR YOU.
SIOUX CITY SUE, SIOUX CITY SUE
THERE AIN'T NO GAL AS TRUE AS MY SWEET SIOUX CITY SUE.
THERE AIN'T NO GAL AS TRUE AS MY SWEET SIOUX CITY SUE.

MABEL. (MILES & CLIVE)
SIOUX CITY SUE (YOU GOTTA LOVE HER)
SIOUX CITY SUE (NO ONE ABOVE HER)
MY HAIR IS BLONDE, MY EYES ARE BLUE.

(CAN'T SEEM TO GET HER OFF MY MIND)

MILES & CLIVE.
THIS GIRL IS REALLY FINE.

MABEL. (MILES & CLIVE)
SIOUX CITY SUE (CAN'T STOP THINKING ABOUT HER)
SIOUX CITY SUE (OH YEAH!)

ALL.
THERE AIN'T NO GAL AS TRUE
AS MY ONE AND ONLY SWEET SIOUX CITY SUE.
WHOO-WHOO-WHOO!

(APPLAUSE LIGHT.
Back on scripts. MABEL bursts into tears.)

ARCHIE. What's wrong, Sue? A young girl like you shouldn't be out in the middle of this blasted waste.
MABEL. It's my fiancé Luke. He's disappeared. I can't find him anywhere.
ARCHIE. You mean, Little Luke, the Pride of Crooked Gulch?
MABEL. Something's happened to him, Joe. Ever since the Pecos Kid told him there was no Santy Claus, he ain't been right.

(ARCHIE/CLIVE/MILES gasp in shock.)

BOYS. No Santy Claus?
MABEL. That's what he said.
ARCHIE. When did Luke disappear?
MABEL. Five days ago. He took every penny he had to buy me a diamond necklace.
BOYS. A diamond necklace?
MABEL. Yes. He said if Santy Claus wasn't going to give me a present, he would.
CLIVE. Was anyone with him?
MABEL. No. He did say something about stopping into the Dead Prospector Saloon to say hello to a friend.

ARCHIE. That friend got a handle?
MABEL. I think he said, Jingle Belle Starlet.
BOYS. Jingle Belle Starlet! *(Group shiver.)*
MABEL. Do you know her?
ARCHIE. Know her? Why, Jingle Belle made us the Lonesome Rangers we are today.

MUSIC INTRO: *"CIGAREETS & WHUSKY"*

(The more straight-out, deadpan the BOYS do this number, the better it works. Think "American Gothic.")

ARCHIE, CLIVE, & MILES.
CIGAREETS AND WHUSKEY, AND WILD WILD WOMEN.
THEY'LL DRIVE YOU CRAZY THEY'LL DRIVE YOU INSANE.
CIGAREETS AND WHUSKEY, AND WILD WILD WOMEN.
THEY'LL DRIVE YOU CRAZY, THEY'LL DRIVE YOU INSANE.

ARCHIE. *(Removes hat.)*
ONCE I WAS HAPPY AND HAD A GOOD WIFE.
I HAD ENOUGH MONEY TO LAST ME FOR LIFE.
I MET WITH A GAL AND WE WENT ON A SPREE.
SHE STARTED MY SMOKING AND DRINKING WHUSKEY.
(Puts on hat.)

ALL.
CIGAREETS AND WHUSKEY, AND WILD WILD WOMEN.
THEY'LL DRIVE YOU CRAZY THEY'LL DRIVE YOU INSANE.
CIGAREETS AND WHUSKEY, AND WILD WILD WOMEN.
THEY'LL DRIVE YOU CRAZY, THEY'LL DRIVE YOU INSANE.

CLIVE. *(Removes hat.)*
NOW I AM FEEBLE AND BROKEN WITH AGE.
THE LINES ON MY FACE MAKE A WELL-WRITTEN PAGE
(Puts on hat.)

MILES. *(Removes hat.)*
I'M LEAVING THIS MESSAGE, HOW SAD BUT HOW TRUE.

MILES & ARCHIE. *(Removes hats.)*
ON CIGAREETS AND WHUSKEY AND WHAT THEY CAN DO.
(Both put on hats.)

ALL.
CIGAREETS AND WHUSKEY, AND WILD WILD WOMEN.
THEY'LL DRIVE YOU CRAZY, THEY'LL DRIVE YOU —

CLIVE. *(Removes hat, speaks.)* — bananas! *(Puts on hat.)*

ALL.
CIGAREETS AND WHUSKEY, AND WILD WILD WOMEN.
THEY'LL DRIVE YOU CRAZY, THEY'LL DRIVE YOU INSANE.

CLIVE. *(Removes hat.)*
SO WRITE ON THE CROSS AT THE HEAD OF MY GRAVE,
(Puts on hat.)

MILES. *(Removes hat.)*
FOR WOMEN AND WHUSKEY HERE LIES A POOR SLAVE.
(Puts on hat.)

ARCHIE. *(Removes hat.)*
TAKE WARNING, DEAR STRANGER,
TAKE WARNING, DEAR FRIEND,

ALL. *(MILES & CLIVE remove hats.)*
AND WRITE IN BOLD LETTERS THESE WORDS AT THE END.

(á capella)
CIGAREETS AND WHUSKEY, AND WILD WILD WOMEN.
THEY'LL DRIVE YOU CRAZY, THEY'LL DRIVE YOU INSANE.

CIGAREETS AND WHUSKEY, AND WILD WILD WOMEN.
THEY'LL DRIVE YOU CRAZY, THEY'LL DRIVE YOU IN—

SAY-YAY-YAY-NE —
(ALL put on hats.)
OOOH.

(APPLAUSE LIGHT.)

MABEL. So you think Little Luke is with this Jingle Belle woman?
ARCHIE. Think? I *know*. We don't have a moment to lose. Come on, boys, saddle up. We're headin' for Crooked Gulch.
(SFX: Horse whinny, furious hoofbeats. Group mimes riding horses.
MUSIC: SEGUE to saloon theme: first lines of UP ON A HOUSE-TOP!
SFX: hoof clops.)

ARCHIE. Here we are in Crooked Gulch — the meanest, dirtiest town in the West. Watch yer step, boys.

(SFX: Step in poop—whoopie cushion.)

ALL. Ew!

(SFX: plunger suction cup sound as they remove foot.)

ARCHIE. And over there's the Dead Prospector Saloon.
CLIVE. *(As GABBY HAYES.)* Cowboy Joe! Cowboy Joe! I seen it all.
ARCHIE. Why, it's Ol' Crusty, the town drunk. Seen what, old feller?
CLIVE. Everything. The crooked card game. The heavy romancin'. She took him, Joe, for everything he had.
MABEL. Oh, no. Where is this Jingle Belle Starlet?
CLIVE. She —

(SFX: gunshot.)

CLIVE. Got me!
ARCHIE. Crusty! You hit?
CLIVE. If I'm not, I got one heck of a case of heartburn.
ARCHIE. Cover me, saddle pals. I'm going in.

(SFX: swinging saloon door; "bump" sound as if it swung back and hit him on the rump.)

MABEL. I'm coming with you.

(SFX: swinging saloon door; "bump" sound as if it swung back and hit her on the rump.)

ARCHIE. Now just a minute. A saloon's no place for a lady.
MABEL. So what's Jingle Belle?

(LESLIE ENTERS in red velvet dress trimmed in white marabou [from Act One, Sc. 1], with wig and Santa hat. Carries script.)

LESLIE. I'm no lady — I'm his wife!

(ARCHIE registers his own real surprise at LESLIE showing up in a dress, then tries to carry on.)

ARCHIE. Jingle Belle!
LESLIE. Joe!
ARCHIE. I see you're still up to your tricks — Belle.
LESLIE. And you're just as charming as ever — Joe.
ARCHIE. Look here, Belle, I don't have time for small talk. Where's Little Luke?
LESLIE. *(Musing)* Little Luke... Little Luke... Short?
ARCHIE. Um-hmm.
LESLIE. Sandy hair?
ARCHIE. Um-hmm.
LESLIE. Big smile and freckles?
ARCHIE. That's Luke.
LESLIE. Never heard of him.
ARCHIE. Now, Jingle Belle, it ain't becoming for you to lie.

MILES. *(Muffled words from behind gag.)* Mmmmphf! Mmmmrrrmmph.
MABEL. Wait, listen! What was that?
MILES. Mmmmphf! Mmmmrrrmmph!
MABEL. Why, that sounds like Luke. He's here!
ARCHIE. Check all the rooms, boys!

(All of the actors mime opening and closing doors, playing straight out to house.
SFX: Door opens; MILES screams like a shocked lady.)

CLIVE. Excuse me.

(SFX: Door slam. Door opens.)

MILES. Do you mind?
ARCHIE. Sorry.

(SFX: Door slam. Door open.)

MILES. Mmmmrrrpmh...

(SFX: Door shut.)

MABEL. Wait a minute! That was Little Luke!

(SFX: Door opens.)

MABEL. Luke! Luke, are you all right? Here, let me untie that gag.
MILES. *(Gasps)* She robbed me, Sue! Of everything.
ALL. Everything?
MILES. *(Nods sadly.)* Everything. My youth, my innocence —
MABEL. Never mind that. What about my diamond necklace?
MILES. That's the one thing she didn't get.
LESLIE. What's this, then?

(LESLIE pulls a glittering necklace out of his bosom. It has a big label that has "FAKE" written on it.)

MILES. A fake.

(MILES displays another necklace whose label reads, "THE REAL THING.")

    LESLIE. What? Why, you —
    ARCHIE. That does it, Belle. I'm taking you in.
    LESLIE. On what charges?
    ARCHIE. *(Ticks off list on fingers.)* Kidnapping. Extortion. *(Looks at LESLIE, adlibs.)* And impersonating a lady.
    LESLIE. You do that, and I'm telling.
    ARCHIE. You're tellin?

(LESLIE nods and cues the band, then walks in a half circle to get in position for:)

MUSIC INTRO:
"I'M GONNA TELL SANTY CLAUS ON YOU"

    CLIVE. Tellin' what?
    MILES. Tellin' who?
    LESLIE. *(Bumps hip at actors, with each "well", they recoil as if bumped.)* Well! Well!

WELL, I'M GONNA TELL SANTY CLAUS ON YOU,
I'M GONNA TELL HIM THAT YOU'VE BEEN UNTRUE.
CHRISTMAS EVE HE'LL KNOW THE SCORE,
HE WON'T COME A-KNOCKING ON YOUR DOOR.

    ARCHIE. What?

    LESLIE.
YOU BETTER NOT TELL HIM YOU'VE BEEN NICE,
GONNA TELL HIM ONCE AND MAYBE TWICE.
HOW YOU BROKE MY HEART IN TWO,
I'M GONNA TELL SANTY CLAUS ON YOU.

NO USE TO HANG YOUR STOCKING ON YOUR
    CHRISTMAS TREE

NO USE TO SIT UP WATCHING FOR SAINT NICK, NO SIREE.

YOU'RE GONNA BE SORRY BY AND BY,
GONNA WAKE UP CHRISTMAS DAY AND CRY.
YOU'LL BE SAD AND I'LL BE BLUE,
I'M GONNA TELL SANTY CLAUS ON YOU.

ARCHIE. Ah, Jingle Belle, listen to me, it ain't true.
LESLIE. You and your Lonesome Rangers. You haven't been lonesome a day in your life.
MABEL. *(To MILES.)* And what about you and that...that...woman?
MILES. Sue!
MABEL. How could you?

MABEL. *(Sings to MILES.)*
WELL, I'M GONNA TELL SANTA CLAUS ON YOU,
GONNA TELL HIM THAT YOU'VE BEEN UNTRUE.

MABEL & LESLIE.
CHRISTMAS EVE, HE'LL KNOW THE SCORE,
HE WON'T COME A-KNOCKIN ON YOUR DOOR.

LESLIE.
YOU BETTER NOT TELL HIM YOU'VE BEEN NICE,

MABEL.
I'LL TELL HIM ONCE AND MAYBE TWICE,
HOW YOU BROKE MY HEART IN TWO.

MABEL & LESLIE.
WE'RE GONNA TELL SANTY CLAUS ON YOU!

(STAN begins playing a swing tom-tom riff reminiscent of "Swing, Swing, Swing" by Benny Goodman, band joins in. LESLIE breaks into a jitterbug dance break, then adds ARCHIE. MILES and MABEL follow suit. CLIVE claps along with STAN. LESLIE and MABEL swing away their partners, and end up together for last verse, a rousing, bump-and-grind final. ARCHIE and MILES throw down hats in "Aw shucks" frustration.)

MABEL & LESLIE.
BUT IF YOU SAY YOU LOVE ME AND PROMISE TO BE
TRUE,
THEN I'LL MAKE A PROMISE THAT I WON'T TELL SANTA
ON YOU.

THEN WE'LL BE HAPPY, YOU AND I,
YOU WON'T BE SAD AND I WON'T CRY.
WE'LL HAVE A MERRY CHRISTMAS, TOO.

MABEL.
'CAUSE I WON'T TELL *(Holds up little finger.)*

LESLIE.
AND I WON'T TELL *(Holds up little finger.)*

MABEL & LESLIE. *(Clasp little fingers in pinkie promise.)*
'CAUSE WE WON'T TELL SANTA CLAUS — ON — YOU!

(APPLAUSE LIGHT.)

MILES. You mean, there really is a Santy Claus?
LESLIE. That's right, honey — and he just loves diamonds.

(LESLIE snatches the real necklace from MILES and turns to exit.)

MABEL. Jingle Belle's getting away!
MILES. Oh, no, she's not.

(SFX: gun cock.)

MILES. *(Mimes drawing gun.)* Freeze, Belle!
LESLIE. Eeeek!
MILES. That necklace belongs to me.

(SFX: gun cock.)

MABEL. *(mimes drawing gun.)* That's what you think.

ALL. *(Reach for the sky.)* Sue!
MABEL. That necklace is mine! You promised.

(SFX: gun cock.)

CLIVE. *(Mimes drawing gun.)* Sorry, Sue, but I'll have to take that off your hands.
ALL. *(Turn and gasp.)* Crusty?
CLIVE. I've waited my whole life for a chance like this.
LESLIE. You'll have to wait a little longer. *(Mimes drawing gun.)*

(SFX: gun cock.)

ALL. *(Turn and gasp.)* Belle!
LESLIE. Fork it over, lamb cakes.

(SFX: Gun cock.)

ARCHIE. *(Mimes drawing gun.)* Stop right there, Jingle Belle.
LESLIE. Joe! You wouldn't!
ARCHIE. Oh, yes, I would. That necklace is a Christmas present and by jingo, I'm going to make sure it's put under a Christmas tree.
LESLIE. Over my dead body. Take that! And that. And — um, that.

(STAN can't find the gunshot stick; gestures helplessly. By the next SFX sequence below, he grabs any effect handy. They are of course inappropriate.)

ARCHIE. *(Covering)* Looks like your gun's jammed, Belle.
LESLIE. Then I'll go for my *back up*. Take — *(SFX: duck call.)* And — *(SFX: whizzer.)* and — *(SFX: horn honk.)*

(LESLIE glares over at STAN, who ducks down under SFX table to hunt for gun stick.)

ARCHIE. They're jammed, too.

(As STAN sorts through the rubble, LESLIE tosses script over his shoulder and starts to improvise. So does ARCHIE.)

LESLIE. Then we'll have to duke it out *mano á mano*. Luckily my hands are registered as deadly weapons.
ARCHIE. *(Improvising)* Ah, but only in the state of Colorado. We're in Arizona, Belle.
LESLIE. Then it's a good thing I'm carrying this stick of dynamite, which I have now lit.

(LESLIE makes hissing sound like fuse.)

ARCHIE. And which I will now put out.

(ARCHIE spits on LESLIE's mimed fuse.)

LESLIE. All right. No more Mr. Nice Guy. Crusty! Hand me the blow gun.
STAN. *(Triumphantly)* I found it!

(STAN fires off a deafening fusillade of shots and first LESLIE, ARCHIE, then ALL sink to the floor as if dead. Silence. The cast lies motionless on the floor for a long, long time. STAN stares at them, stunned at what has happened.
Important note: no one should move a muscle. If STAN or any of the band tries to "fill" the moment or reacts with more than one take, the comic tension is lost. Focus must be kept on the actors on the floor. Trust this bit: it works!
Finally ARCHIE lifts his head.)

ARCHIE. Erm. Whose line is it?
MILES. *(Lifts head.)* Not me — I'm dead.
MABEL. *(Lifts head.)* I'm dead.
CLIVE. *(Lifts head.)* I'm dead, too.
LESLIE. *(Lifts head.)* You mean, we're all dead?

(ALL turn heads as one and glare at STAN.)

STAN. Oops.

(ARCHIE snaps fingers and cues band; from their positions on the floor, the cast sings RAGTIME COWBOY JOE, getting to their feet and moving into position around the mike.)

ALL.
HE ALWAYS SINGS
RAGGY MUSIC TO THE CATTLE AS HE SWINGS
BACK AND FORWARD IN THE SADDLE ON A HORSE
THAT IS SYNCOPATED GAITED
AND IT'S SUCH A FUNNY METER
TO THE ROAR OF HIS REPEATER.

(They "dooby-do" the rest of the tune under MABEL's lines.)

MABEL. *(Into mike.)* Er — be sure to tune in next time for another exciting adventure with Cowboy Joe and his Lonesome Rangers — as they learn all about their new life in, er, uh...

(The singing stops.)

MABEL. Cowboy heaven!

(MUSIC kicks in.)

ALL.
COWBOY!

ARCHIE. That's me!

ALL.
COWBOY!

ARCHIE. See ya next time!

ALL.
RAGTIME COWBOY —

(A loud commotion is heard just outside SL door.)

VOICES OFF. Open up! We gotta a show to do. What the heck's goin' on here, Tex? Don't know, Slappy. But I'm sure gonna find out.

(CLIVE crosses, glances out the door, and ducks back in a panic.)

    CLIVE. Good heavens! It's the cowboys. The *real* cowboys.
    MILES. What do we do?
    LESLIE. Hide!

(LESLIE leaps into audience; the others come together in a panicked huddle. They whisper intently, keeping the tension up until the decision to finish the show is reached.)

    VOICES OFF. Hey! Open up in there.
    MABEL. Oh, boy. Tex is really gonna be mad.
    ARCHIE. Then we'd better let 'im in.

(ARCHIE goes to open the door.)

    MILES. Stop!
    ARCHIE. Sorry?
    MILES. Don't open that door!
    CLIVE. Miles, are you mad? We have to let them in.
    ARCHIE. It *is* their show, you know.
    MILES. No. It's not. It's *our* show.
    MABEL. Our show?
    MILES. Yes. Ours. *(Runs to SL door and bars it with a broom handle.)* When the chips were down, who stepped up to the mark and shouldered on? *We* did. By George, even the blitz couldn't stop us.
    ARCHIE. And we bloody well pulled it off, too.
    VOICES OFF. Okay. What's goin' on in there? Come on, let us in!
    MABEL. *(Torn)* If I don't open that door, Tex'll fire me for sure. But if I open it, I'm back in the booth again.

ARCHIE. And you deserve more than that, Mabel.
MILES. Much more.
CLIVE. Much, *much* more.
LESLIE. Indeed.
MABEL. Thanks, fellas. You sure are swell. Well, there's only one song left in the show. I say we do it.
ARCHIE. I'm with Mabel. Clive?
CLIVE. I'm game.
ARCHIE. Miles?
MILES. Count me in.
ARCHIE. Leslie?
LESLIE. I suppose it's only polite to ask the audience what they think.

(ALL glance at house.)

LESLIE. But let's not press our luck. It's time to saddle up — and ride!
ALL. YEE-HAW!

MUSIC INTRO:
"ROVIN' COWBOY/RIDE, COWBOY, RIDE FINALE"

MABEL. *(Into mike.)* Well, folks, thanks for being with us tonight. It sure has been one wild holiday stampede.
LESLIE. *(At mike.)* Indeed. I think I may safely say that the programme you've just witnessed was unlike any ever presented in the history of the BBC.
MILES. *(At mike.)* Well put, Leslie. And on behalf of all of us here at Broadcasting House, Happy Christmas, and farewell until next time —
MABEL. *Next* time?
LESLIE. You never know.

(ARCHIE & CLIVE join LESLIE, MABEL & MILES at mikes.)

ARCHIE. *(Sings)*
HEAR MY SONG AS I RIDE ALONG,

ALL.
I'M JUST A HAPPY ROVIN' COWBOY,
HERDIN' THE DARK CLOUDS OUT OF THE SKY,
KEEPIN' THE HEAVENS BLUE.

LESLIE.
I AIN'T GOT A WIFE TO BOTHER MY LIFE,
I'M A HAPPY ROVING COWBOY.

ARCHIE.
LET ME MAKE MY BED WHERE THE VARMINTS PROWL
BENEATH THE SKY OF BLUE.

ALL.
HEAR MY SONG AS I RIDE ALONG,
I'M JUST A HAPPY ROVIN' COWBOY.
HERDIN' THE DARK CLOUDS OUT OF THE SKY,
KEEPIN' THE HEAVENS BLUE.

COME ON AND RIDE, COWBOY, RIDE.
ROLL UP YOUR REATAS AND PULL YOUR SOMBREROS
DOWN TIGHT.
WE'RE GOING TO RIDE, RIDE, RIDE,
WHERE THE TRAIL WILL WIND.
YOU BETTER DRIVE, DRIVE, DRIVE
OR WE'LL LEAVE YOU BEHIND.
COME ON AND RIDE — RIDE — RIDE — COWBOY, RIDE.

CLIVE.
I AIN'T GOT A DIME, I'M JUST SPENDING MY TIME,
I'M A HAPPY ROVING COWBOY.

MILES & MABEL.
LET ME RIDE THAT LONG TRAIL DOWN TO THE END
WHERE THE SKIES ARE ALWAYS BLUE.

ALL.
HEAR MY SONG AS I RIDE ALONG,
I'M JUST A HAPPY ROVIN' COWBOY.

HERDIN' THE DARK CLOUDS OUT OF THE SKY,
KEEPIN' THE HEAVENS BLUE.

CLIVE.
IT'S A BEAUTIFUL MORNIN' AND YOU'VE HAD A GOOD REST,

MILES.
YOU ROPERS, GET READY TO BE AT YOUR BEST.

MABEL.
RIDE INTO TOWN AND FIND A LADY OR TWO,

ALL.
TO TAKE YOU BY THE ARMS
AND SHAKE THAT DUST OFF YOUR BOOTS.
COME — ON — AND —
(CAST breaks into kick line.)
RIDE, COWBOY, RIDE!
(Back to regular tempo.)
ROLL UP YOUR REATAS AND PULL YOUR SOMBREROS DOWN TIGHT.
WE'RE GOING TO RIDE, RIDE, RIDE,
WHERE THE TRAIL WILL WIND.
YOU BETTER DRIVE, DRIVE, DRIVE
OR WE'LL LEAVE YOU BEHIND.
COME ON AND RIDE — RIDE — RIDE — COWBOY, RIDE!

ALL. *(Shout, wave hats.)* Merry Christmas!

BLACK OUT

END OF PLAY

PROPERTIES LIST

4 vintage microphones w/ stands
Tea pot
Tea cup/saucer
Small spoon
Tea bags
2 hip flasks
7 copies of script pages
Steamer trunk
Large metal spoon (off L)
Tall stool
Tall lectern (wheeled)
3 wooden chairs
2 long tables
1 side table
Small roll/gaffers tape (Archie)
Brief case
Applause light
2 clipboards
Ventriloquist's dummy
Tall folding screen
Muslin dummy body
Broom (UL corner)
Medium stool (Stan)
4-5 wrapped presents (one should open and have a Santa hat inside)
Christmas decorations

COSTUME PROPERTIES

Round glasses (Clive)
Round glasses, shattered (Clive, Act II)
Bowler (Leslie)
Chef's hat (Leslie)
White apron (Leslie)
5 pair chaps (All)
5 pair boots (All)
Watch (Miles)
Watch (Mabel)
Small cowboy hat (Miles)
Small cowboy outfit (Miles — preset on dummy)
Gas mask pack (Stan)
Ten-gallon hat (Clive)
Boa (Leslie)
Drag costume (Leslie)
Small tool belt (Archie)
WWI war helmet (Stan)
Half-glasses (Leslie)

Exciting New Musicals From Our Catalogue!

OPEN HEART
Book, Music, & Lyrics by Robby Benson

The primetime television sitcom business of making America laugh is a cut-throat industry swarming with abundant greed, deceit and deliciously evil players, and of course the naïve, yet creative, buffoon who wants to change the world. Life can become a canceled sitcom if one is not careful. 2m, 1f (#17743)

"A sharp, uncompromising look at the value of true love ... sad, happy and satisfied all at the same time." — broadway.com

GORILLA MAN
Book, Music, & Lyrics by Kyle Jarrow

Puberty is hard enough without the insatiable thirst for blood! Waking one morning to find thick fur growing on the backs of his hands, young Billy discovers the awful truth his mother has been hiding from him for fourteen years: he's destined to grow up into a murderous monster. Cast from his home, he sets out on a journey to find his father, the legendary Gorilla Man. Combining a variety influences including horror films, picaresque tales, and glam rock, GORILLA MAN is a strikingly original new musical, a pulse-pounding mix of comedy, concert, and carnival that explores philosophical issues of identity, ethics, and free will. 3m, 2f, 2 m or f (#9929)

"Big, bloody, ridiculous theatricality ... There's a unity of vision and insanity that's exciting." — *The New York Sun*

THE BASIC CATALOGUE OF PLAYS AND MUSICALS
online at www.samuelfrench.com